T0062432

"Through the Door!"

"Through the Door!"

A Journey to the Self

Phil L. Méthot
Trafford Publishing
Bloomington, In, U.S.A. 47403

Order this book online at www.trafford.com
or email orders@trafford.com

Most Trafford titles are also available at major online book retailers.

© Copyright 2010 Phil L. Méthot .
All rights reserved. No part of this publication may be reproduced, stored in a retrieval system, or
transmitted, in any form or by any means, electronic, mechanical, photocopying, recording, or
otherwise, without the written prior permission of the author.

Printed in Victoria, BC, Canada.

ISBN: 978-1-4269-1711-0 (sc)

ISBN: 978-1-4269-2376-0 (hc)

*Our mission is to efficiently provide the world's finest, most comprehensive book publishing
service, enabling every author to experience success. To find out how to publish your book, your
way, and have it available worldwide, visit us online at www.trafford.com*

Trafford rev. 1/6/2010

www.trafford.com

North America & international
toll-free: 1 888 232 4444 (USA & Canada)
phone: 250 383 6864 ♦ fax: 812 355 4082

Acknowledgements

So many people influence your life and steer you in directions that you may not have had the courage to go. My case is no exception. Two very special people challenged my limitations. They did not let me buy into a view of self that would have kept me in misery all my life. Those two people were George Raynault and Nell Thomson. To them I have a debt that I could never pay back.

I am indebted to Hampton Roads Publishing Co. for their permission to include excerpts from Neale Donald Walsch's book; Conversations with God, Book 2, 1997

The photo of me on the About the Author page was taken by Ryan Millward of Montreal.

To my children Mandara, Maya, and Kalindi, whose gifts to me was their presence in my life.

To James, my step-son who became so much more.

To my parents for giving me my unique world-view, it taught me immeasurably.

Finally, to Linda my wife who has provided me with laughter, love, and the best friend a person could ask for.

"Toto, I've a feeling we're not in Kansas anymore."
Dorothy Gale; The Wizard of Oz

Contents

Preface

The path to the completion of this book was far from a straight line. Soon after starting, "Through the Door!", I was placed in the fortunate position of accepting a contract as a lecturer aboard a cruise ship in the Caribbean. Every week more than one thousand new people entered upon my stage, and I had the front row seat. As people came and went, I was able to view the ideas I was working on from the perspective of many cultures.

Maybe more than the passengers, the staff and crew of the ship offered a laboratory rich and vibrant in its diversity. When so many cultures conglomerate, both their similarities and differences become striking.

From a behavioural point of view, the hierarchies based on position, race and experience, mixed in with individual self-concepts, provided a rich background from which to study.

Although I would coin the term "self-image Paradox" much later, I was witnessing the phenomenon on a daily basis. I could see it demonstrated in the individuals I studied. Their words and body language were telling me that something else was going on.

One day, while watching some crewmates playing a game of basketball, I turned to a passenger beside me and said:

"Watch the big guy. Within ten minutes he is going to fall down and hurt himself and have to leave the game."

When that event happened in seven minutes, I was just as impressed as the passenger next to me. It had not occurred to me the extent that I had integrated what I was seeing. When I made the original comment to the bystander, I wasn't quite sure where it had come from. Only after the fact did I realize that what I had seen in the basketball player's eyes and body language was the realization that he could not keep up with the other players. Something also told me that his self-image could not allow him to admit physical defeat. The accident solved both problems because now he had a valid, face-saving reason to leave the game. I know that the player never for a moment would believe that he had set himself up to 'accidentally' trip like that.

"THROUGH THE DOOR!"

It was at this very moment that I knew there was an important story to tell. How many decisions do we make based on what we think is going on, while a hidden motive goes unnoticed? How often do we react to events or conversations based on subtle unconscious self-images that keep us repeating patterns of behaviour that have long since lost their value?

As a motivational management consultant, I helped companies make changes to their corporate culture that immediately produced positive results in company morale and improved bottom line. My work inspired wonderful letters of appreciation from their C.E.O.'s Far too often, however, I witnessed relapses into previous behaviour that nullified the all the great gains that had been made. The patterns of behaviour that ensued seemed to have more to do with the self-images I perceived of the senior managers and how that played out on the company stage. This confirmed in my mind that our self-images play a much greater role in our personal and professional lives, and indeed, affect every aspect of our society. It seemed clear to me that there was quite a difference between the images we have of ourselves, and who we really are. I realized that unconscious ideas played a far greater role in our daily behaviour than most people realize. Furthermore, I believed that these unconscious behaviours could be known, understood and changed. Before this could happen I needed to be able to understand certain questions in a way that we could all understand and use. What are the processes that go into defining who we are? Why do our images of our selves differ so much from what we really are? What forces are at work that compels us to repeat behaviours that are counter to our desires?

I was not interested in knowing what we can find in books on psychology. If the information wasn't in the minds of everyday man or woman, then the information wasn't accessible. What I felt we needed was an understanding of our behaviour that could be grasped by everyone, and furthermore allow some sort of mechanism by which we could choose to alter our patterns of behaviour to bring about the results we want.

This book is a result of asking basic questions and then looking at the answers. Why do people do so many things that seem to cause more problems? Are some people in truth self-destructive or is there something else going on? What if we are in fact smarter, wiser, and more capable then our behaviours suggests. What, then, would be the reasons for our apparent crazy behaviour? I believe that this book will answer those questions.

I wrote this book with the following intentions:

- To expose our self-images as the fragile beasts that they are.
- To show that there are actually three different processes that go on that we call self-image.
- To illustrate that language has played a big part in keeping us where we are.
- To thoroughly introduce the master and commander of the ship...our Will.
- To give us the power to place our goals and desires where they belong – in that part of the mind that takes real action.

I believe that the outcome of this book will be, for many of you, a turning point in life; not because the book is magical, but because you are. This book will demonstrate it without any doubt.

3:00 am

It is curious to note that night-time oft brings,
Words and ideas of daytime things.
I awake with a phrase, or only a word,
Reflections of daytime musings heard
.

Then, as the night time tutelage begins,
Words drive through my head, like heat-driven winds.
Like the milkweed pod that explodes,
The words rush out fast – the mind reloads.
What tutor, what mystic, whence do they come?
These answers, these gifts, this ancient wisdom?

Oh night time awakening, thy message so deep,
Transforming my being, so far now from sleep.
As to the creator – an author unknown.
But this vessel's indebted for what I've been shown.
Its message so simple, I espouse it to you,
Let that which you are, be that which you do.

Phil L. Méthot

Introduction

Is it possible to make complete, awe-inspiring, changes in our lives? Do we need to have calamitous near-death experiences before we decide that our life can be so very different than is it today? We have heard of people pulled from fires, or rescued from drowning who, after the experience, turned their lives around and started living their dreams. We have tended to see these individuals as heroes, and maybe in a sense they are, for stories of people who changed their lives in mid-journey to achieve something that would have been unthinkable for them before, do inspire us. Hearing these stories often creates enough tension within us so that we stop ourselves in our tracks and say:

"Hey, I don't want to be like this anymore!"

Why do we need to wait for an external monumental event to come crashing over our heads? Why do we need such a strong force to push us to live life the way we would truly desire? Wouldn't it be better to acknowledge that we are not living our desires and then take the steps required without pushing ourselves to the edge first?

Why is it that some simple acts seem to be so hard to do? Things such as being too shy to ask someone to dance, or asking a question in an audience, or even talking to an audience. Why do these situations create such fears in us? We certainly are not in any danger in these situations, yet we react as if our lives were in peril. Just being able to do these acts without sweating would make a huge impact in our lives and reduce a great percentage of the stress we feel in any given day. It is easy to say, "Don't sweat the small stuff", but in fact we do spend most of our time and energy in dealing with the small stuff. At the time that we are in it, it does not seem like small stuff at all! The cumulative stress of wondering if you are too tall, too short, too skinny, etc, takes such a toll that the very idea of changing the big stuff becomes unthinkable. So much so that many people have unfortunately bought into the idea that, "people don't change".

Let's find the underlying cause of this, shall we? Let's look at what is really going on so that it makes sense to you. We are going to explore the idea of the self. What do we mean when we say, myself? You have an image of yourself that changes all the time. When you slip and fall in front of others, you may see yourself as clumsy. Your image of yourself first thing in the morning is an image that you would often keep to yourself. When you are wearing your best outfit, you may see yourself more positively. Whom you see yourself as changes with circumstances, so is it *you* that really changes or the image you have of yourself? Your idea of "self" is dependent on several things. Actually, three separate processes go into the creation of your idea of self, and we will reveal them shortly. Suffice it to say, you possess not a self-image, but many self-images and what makes one appear instead of others results in the quality of life that you live every day. Some self-images show up as a habit, and like smoking, can seriously affect your quality of life. Rather than reaching for your pack of "shyness", or lighting up guilt, let me show you how you can quit the habit of puffing on unwanted self-images.

This is a layperson's guide, a poet's view if you will. You will still be able to recognize the sense and science of it without it being crammed down your throat. The word "educate" in its root meaning, means, "To bring out." Therefore, it is the intent of this book to knock on your door and ask you if you want to come out to play. Rather than having to stay inside to do your homework, I ask you to come, "Through the Door", and witness the world, your world, the way it should be for you. Not the way anyone tells you it should be, but the way the world makes sense to you. To do this, we will remove the blindfold that self-images place over your senses, and show you what your longings have been about all this time.

Those of you, who remember the movie "The Wizard of Oz", based on the book by Frank L. Baum, will remember the scene when Dorothy trapped in her house comes crashing down in Oz. The scene is entirely in black and white until she opens the door and steps out into the Land of Oz, which is incredibly colourful. As a child watching that movie, (and new to colour TV), I was awestruck at the change from black and white to colour. So years later, when I tried to explain to someone the profound changes possible in their life when they invoked their Will, the image that came into my mind was that of

INTRODUCTION

Dorothy going through the door and entering the sensual splendour of Oz; hence the title for this book.

I invite you all to come and see the great and powerful wizard who resides in your mind, just waiting for you to ask for courage, or a brain, or a heart. You always had the ability to go home, (that place within that shows you that almost anything is possible); all you needed was to have someone explain it to you.

Therefore, ladies and gentlemen, I invite you...

..."Through the Door!"

1

Me, Myself, and I

There is nothing so misunderstood as the concept of self-image.
People go through enormous lengths to find it. They spend countless
dollars buying books by those who would tell them what to do to get
in touch with it, improve it, make peace with it, love it, and so on. It is
a curious irony that many of those who seek to find their self-image do
so outside of themselves. It would seem that the very act of seeking
tends to obscure the self, for the search for something reflects the
belief that one does not possess it. It is much like the absent-minded
individual who looks for his eyeglasses without realizing that he is
wearing them. As long as he searches "out there", he cannot find what
is right in front of his eyes.

Yet the search goes on for this "quality" called the self, which has
no shape, cannot be touched or pointed to, yet sets off so many people
on journeys to discover it. Some of the greatest stories ever written
dealt with heroes and heroines who left all behind to wander through
physical, emotional, or spiritual journeys in order to crack the illusory
cocoon that surrounded them. Some of the world's great religions were
created because of these very personal searches. Empires were built,
lands discovered, and works of art created as individuals sought
themselves, and changed the world in the process.

A most curious paradox concerns not the need to find the self, but
the notion that the self is lost in the first place. Who is doing the search
if it isn't our self? What is it that we think could disappear from us so
that we would feel absent from ourselves? How can we solve the
paradox that if we are feeling absent, we have to be the ones feeling
absent, and therefore must be there in order to feel it!

A standard question given to students of philosophy concerns the
possibility of an omnipotent god who could create something so heavy
that even "he" couldn't lift it. After some hours of debating, it would
be pointed out that the solution to the problem lies in the
understanding that linguistically, the sentence itself is flawed and the

"language" does not make sense. So too in the question of finding the self, the problem is in the question. As to the self-image, the thing searched is always the searcher. This statement does not diminish the pain or sense of loss that one may have inside, but it clarifies that fact that one had better find out exactly what is missing if one wishes to find it.

The fellow with the glasses on his head can never solve the problem because the glasses aren't lost. The problem is something else entirely. When we understand what goes on in our life that causes us to feel disconnected from ourselves, we then have the capacity to solve the problem.

The very self that is doing the search is not lost nor is it undeveloped. The urge to find it is actually a call from it yelling at us:

"Hey, I'm right here…no, here, Right here, no, wait, come back… I'm

right here…!"

The detachment we feel from ourselves reflects the difference we intuitively understand between what we are living and who we are. Whom do we think is urging us to find ourselves? To have such a sense of this distance is of itself an indication that we possess the knowledge of what we should be (by our own inner self's criteria), or else we could not feel the distance from it. It tells us that our lives as we are living them are not reflecting this inner sense of self. That self is not lost. Rather, it is telling us that it is right there for us to access.

A great part of the problem, which causes us to miss the messages that we give ourselves, has to do with the nature of "language" itself. Language has its origin and its greatest function in tribal or cultural survival. This is reflected in the many languages and regional dialects found in the world where the needs in one community are different from the next. Over centuries, languages developed variations based on the types of situations that needed expressing in the various groups.

Since the complexities of tribal life necessitated the need for more complex expressions, language developed to satisfy these needs.

ME, MYSELF, AND I

Language was therefore an expression of the needs of the group rather than that of the individual. This is so obstinately true even today that in several languages, English and French included, there is no single pronoun for the third person singular. When we write, we always have that awkward "him or her", or, "he or she", because there is no one word for a general person who is non-gender specific. It still is not important enough in our society that the English language require a word to indicate the individual when speaking in the third person. This has much to do with the original cultural positioning of females as "unequal" to males, but also shows the evolutionary dismissal of the individual, male or female, as an important entity.

English is a very evolved and evolving language. We have seen the ease with which new words have entered into the Oxford English Dictionary, such as Homer Simpson's "D'oh", and the hip-hop version of jewellery, "bling". Yet after all this time, there is no single word to identify an individual in general. The silence of the language is telling.

If we are going to try to understand our self-image dilemma, let us look at the words for their meaning, and see if that matches our experience. We do not often reflect in our day-to-day lives upon our own speech. It is mostly an automatic process and therefore most of what we say does not provoke critical introspection. As language is the medium of the tribe, then it should seem natural that language would favour expressions that are more in keeping with a group's consciousness.

Careful monitoring of our daily speech shows us that we are often hesitant to "own" our words. We say things such as; "You go to a store and get lousy service, and you feel angry!" What we are really saying is; "I went to a store and got lousy service, and so I was angry!" Even when it comes to writing a résumé, where the intent is to sell ourselves to a future employer and it is obvious that we are talking about ourselves, we deem it inappropriate to use the first person and state boldly that:

"I was promoted to management after only three weeks on the job."

No, we are tacitly encouraged to create incomplete sentences and say something such as:

3

"THROUGH THE DOOR!"

"Was promoted to management after only three weeks on the job."

We seemingly avoid the notion that we may actually be talking about ourselves, even when that is the intent of a conversation or written communication. The injunction to stand up and "be counted" is quite noticeable in our western civilization and much of this is due, I believe, to the reinforcement of language as a tribal device.

This being the case, then maybe what you are saying when attempting to "speak your mind" is not always a direct translation of what you would really say if the tribal urge wasn't present. It is possible, therefore, for you to say one thing, while what you really mean is something else. The question that this brings up is; "Does your mind, which makes pictures in your head with the words it hears, act on the words, or the 'intent' behind them?" For example, could it be that a person " starving for affection" may only hear the message, "starving" and consequently feed the wrong impulse?

Our minds will try to deal with a verbal message even if it does not really represent what we are feeling underneath. It becomes clear that we need to be sure that our words reflect what we really mean, especially when it comes to knowing what we want to be and do.

Since language itself shares the blame in the suppression of the individual, we need to examine exactly what we mean when we say self-image. There are actually three separate processes occurring that have, as a result, the capacity to produce an "image" of ourselves in relation to the rest of the world. We make no distinction between these processes in our everyday language and consequently we group them into that concept called self-image. Each one affects our behaviour differently and as such; we must then look at these three processes and separate them clearly in our minds.

We will deal with each one in separate chapters and see the weight that each one has on determining our "natural" inclinations.

Briefly, though, we will say that the three systems stem from:
- Our relation to the environment.
- Our relation to "the tribe".
- Our relation to our self.

In each of these three processes, the only one that reflects our true self-image is the last one – our relation to our self. There are no problems with this system because it is a true reflection of who we are. Our relation to the environment produces images of our self in the same way as other animals. Our relation to the tribe produces a uniquely human view of the self, one that has the least to do with who we actually are.

Regardless of which system has produced the self-image, generally when we say "my self-image," we refer to something integrated within us. It becomes "us". We speak of the images we have of ourselves as if we were discussing our arm or leg. We say such things as; "I'm shy", not "I have shyness." We say; "I am embarrassed", not "I have embarrassment." So let us acknowledge, then, that our self-images are more likened to an extension of us, like a body part rather than that of a piece of clothing that we can change on a daily basis. We accept our self-images, some albeit reluctantly, and live our lives through their influences.

The "shy" person, for example, lives by the rules of "shyness". Shyness has a certain pattern of behaviour, and an inner directive motivates the shy person to live under that pattern. We all know the patterns and have no problem picking out the shy person in a room. As we have said, we do not distinguish among the three processes that create self-images. We do not even have the language that allows us to discuss the different processes, hence to us, there are all the same. This has important even crucial consequences in how we live our lives.

We will see how one of these systems in particular controls most of our daily behaviour. So much so that for most people, it would seem that there is little hope ever in just being you. Fear not. We have all experienced in our lives that "aha" moment where we decide to change a behaviour that no longer represents who we are. This may even happen in spite of the social environment that pressures us to conform.

This is exactly the point where there should be a distinction made and a word given to describe the differences among the three systems. Only in this way can a person make distinctions between what is their idea of self versus adopted ideas of self. Without the words, there is no concept, and without the concept, the difference remains hidden.

As far back as 1901, Dr. Richard Maurice Bucke, A Canadian psychologist lauded by the father of American Psychiatry, William James, made a profound statement. In his book, Cosmic Consciousness, he stated; "No word can come into being except as the expression of a concept, neither can a new concept be formed without the formation (at the same time) of the new word which is its expression, though this 'new word' may be spelled and pronounced as is some old word." (Bucke, 1901)

In other words, language is born from the need to express concepts. Concepts demand of us a name. When we give several concepts the same name, then the understanding of these concepts become diluted in our mind.

For example: wonderful, exuberant, elated, contented, ecstatic, joyful, thrilled, pleased, blissful, ebullient, jovial, and enraptured all encompass a variation of the experience that is grouped into the word mostly used today – happy. Even though we have the capacity to distinguish the subtleties of all of these versions of happiness, without the words in our vocabulary, these subtleties go unnoticed. You would be hard-pressed to find people who sense the difference between these emotions in their daily lives, even if they know the words. If they are not a part of our regular vocabulary, then the mind seemingly does not make us conscious of the differences.

By grouping the three systems mentioned under the concept self-image, we have lost our grasp of the differences, and consequently the ability to distance ourselves for the most part, with the ideas of our self than those that came from outside of us.

If, as Bucke says, concepts must have a word created for them by using the same words for the same experience, we cease to notice the difference.

Thus, we have the situation where we think of our self-image as that which results from our personal decisions, as well as the automatic acceptance of external influences from nature and from the tribe, as our own. A break-up of the three concepts must occur in order to conceptualize the power of choice and therefore create the ability to look consciously at those behaviours we wish to change.

Once the division occurs and the concept understood, the real power to change begins. In many instances, there is a subtlety to language and the difference between what we say and what we desire to express may be hidden within a little word. For example, I have never heard anyone say, "I have to take out my garbage." They always say that they are taking out "the" garbage. Garbage is not something that people speak of in terms of ownership, even though they have generated it. It's always, "the garbage." Consequently, no one feels a great sense of loss putting it out in the street to be taken away.

The difference here between "the" and "my", though seemingly arbitrary, changes the concept and accordingly our emotional relationship to garbage completely. One makes it a thing, a lump, something that is over there and in the way; the other makes it a thing that demands responsibility. One does not take out the garbage with the idea of civil responsibility, (even if it is true); one takes it out because it stinks, and it is in the way.

When we think of some of the images we have of ourselves, we certainly don't have any problems admitting that some of our images don't help us at all and, in fact, stink and can be quite debilitating. Yet we are not able to say:

"Well this image of me is garbage; I'll just throw it away."

How wonderful it could be if we could take our doubts, low esteems, unworthy, unlovable self-images, and call the city to come and pick them up at the curb!

We can learn a lot by looking at our language for clues to the way we think of ourselves and how we hold onto those ideas, both as individuals, and as a group. Part of the solution is in the reclassification of concepts that we value regarding the self, and to do so at a core level, such that the natural inclination will just be to toss out unwanted images as garbage.

Hence, a greater consciousness of the way in which we speak is an important step, as well as the consciousness of the self-talk or meta-talk that goes on continuously in our head. The greatest clues of our own enslavement to these ineffective self-images can be found in the dialogue that no one else hears but us.

Likewise, in conversations with others, people will respond to our words even if we ourselves are not paying attention to what we are saying. Let's then look at the language of self-image in a different way and see if we can extract the power to "take out the garbage", and then fill up the space with that which we want.

2

Where Did I Go?

Here is an interesting concept to ponder. You are in front of this book right now, looking at the words on this page. What you are looking at are my thoughts when I was putting them down. So in fact, you are looking at past thoughts. As you read this, you sense that I am talking to you right now, even though I wrote this quite some time ago. I don't know your name or when you are reading this, and I can't see you; however, to you it feels that I am talking directly to you and I'm doing it now. In fact, many people are reading this at different times, all with the same feeling. There is only one of you to you, but many of you to me. Even though this is a present event for you, from my point of view, it is a past experience. Furthermore, even though to you this is a two-person event, i.e., the writer and the reader, from the writer's point of view it is a multiple event over multiple times!

The events in our lives, it seems, are rarely as simple as they might appear. We see that reading a book is a complex combination of time and seemingly multiple events. One reads as if he or she is the only reader, while the writer writes hopefully to a multitude of people.

Our past experiences likewise are always intermingling themselves into our present experiences so that our present is intertwined by our past. Here is another example of this enigma. At whatever stage of life you are at when you are reading this book, you have had various stages before this. You have been a baby, toddler, son/daughter, adolescent, teenager, student, and from there, many possible paths such as labourer, professional, significant other, and on and on to the various avenues of life that you have followed. Each one of these stages developed areas of your personality and these personalities were appropriate to the stage you experienced.

When you changed your situation by growing up, moving, graduating, working, etc. these personalities did not entirely disappear. You still have elements of the person who was sent to their room for "being bad." You're the little one who loved to be cuddled. You're the one who took tantrums when you didn't get your way, and you are the one who sometimes felt too embarrassed to answer even the simplest questions. You are the one who revelled in a job well done; you are the teenager who knew everything whilst your parents knew nothing.

The youngster in you who jumped and screamed with excitement when you won a race still shows up whenever your team scores at the basketball or baseball game you are watching. The language of arguments is still replete with phrases and tones of selves gone by. When talking or playing with little children, it is as if a child in you comes out to play and can be seen in your actions and words. Therefore, these self-images, created in the past, are present today, wielding a certain percentage of your present responses to situations.

As you look out your one pair of eyes, the you that is looking is influenced by the sum of the whole team of images of yourself, each seeing the world in the present through their own interpretation of what life was like at their stage in creation. While it appears that, whatever action you take will seem like the actions of one individual, all of these selves have a chance to whisper in your ear their point of view on what action you should take for any given event out there.

Each image would like to take a crack at the situation in progress and handle it the way it sees fit. All one has to do to witness this is to go to karaoke one night at the local bar. Watch the faces of the audience for visible proof of the battle that goes on inside a person as the different personalities battle for the decision to stay in the chair or to go up on stage and sing.

You can pick one individual and watch the following: The kid inside that wants to be noticed is restless in the seat saying, "I wanna turn, I wanna turn." Then, another child, in the same body, sits as far back in the chair as possible, and you can see by the expression on his or her face the fear that; "They're going to laugh at me!" Meanwhile, the young adult in residence steps in saying, "There is no way I'm going to make a fool of myself in front of everyone!" We are not talking about different people here, but a single individual going through all the different possibilities in their head. Meanwhile all these selves show up on his or her face!

WHERE DID I GO?

What transpires to the keen observer is a chair ballet choreographed by the self-images in the mind as each takes its turn as director. Whichever self-image emerges as the winner, it will still hear the others voicing their disapproval of its action.

Most times the self-image that supersedes the others and causes us to behave in a certain way is the appropriate image, "appropriate" being defined here merely as the behaviour we want to exhibit. Sometimes, however, a certain image of our self comes out at very inappropriate times and causes us all sorts of difficulty.

You have experienced times in your adult life where the appropriate response to a question would have been to say, "No", but the child image in you, afraid of being disliked, said, "Yes." You have seen yourself attracted to someone and just when it was the opportune time to say something to break the ice, the awkward teenager or the shy child in you lost courage, and you remained silent. You have had critical times in your life when fear, shame, embarrassment, or cowardice sprang up when least expected and foiled your attempt to do what seemed appropriate at the time. You recognized the behaviour often-just moments after it appeared.

You may make comments such as, "I can't believe I said that," or, "Why did I do that?" and even, "What's wrong with me?" You have even tried to stop yourself before saying something you didn't want to say. You're standing in front of someone and you are screaming at yourself in your mind:

"Shut up…don't you dare…don't say it….", and the next thing you know, you've said exactly what you didn't want to say. It sure did feel like someone in you wanted to say it, but it wasn't you!

On the long-term scale, you have seen yourself hate the job you are in, or have been in relationships for years that have not been satisfying, or have had ideas or projects that have been simmering on the back burner without ever getting the chance to be expressed. Unrealized ambitions and desires punish you with the reminder that they still are there and waiting. You create elaborate reasons to justify the need to keep these desires and dreams at bay.

Most of these reasons seem quite legitimate, and most of your friends would agree with you that these reasons are indeed facts that you cannot ignore. In this way, they give you the support for staying exactly as you are. These same "reasons", however, are impulses created by self-images who were themselves created when you were much younger and without the capacities that you acquired later in life.

The Birth of the Lost Self

When the inappropriate self-image starts to dominate too much of our lives such that much of our daily activity no longer represents us now, but combinations of personalities we have been in the past, we start to feel lost, and our sense of self is greatly diminished. An example would be a person who believes that they are unlovable. This image of self, certainly caused by external forces, can completely dominate a person's response to life, limiting it severely. This can occur in spite of the fact that this self-image is not representative of the individual's true nature.

This, then, is the incubation of the idea of the lost self. Those compelling urges that have sparked philosophies, and may indeed have created philosophy itself, found their birth here. The search for self, therefore, is the attempt to find a way of allowing our self to respond appropriately to our inner drives without eliciting the self-images that are afraid of letting us have our way.

This depiction of the human mind could make everyone sound schizophrenic. However, it is the mind responding in its most natural way based on the way it developed. We, as humans, have as a trade-off for self-consciousness and choice, overridden a lot of the learned behaviour, witnessed so readily in other animals.

Our patterns are still intact, but there is that other part of our mind, which runs on free choice, that always gives us the ability to override these learned traits. It is this part of the mind that lets us bungee jump off a bridge. All the fears which would assail most individuals merely thinking of jumping into thin air with a rubber band strapped around their legs, is overridden when the desire for a thrill or sense of accomplishment is stronger than the fear inside. What is a thrill if it is not the feeling of doing something that goes against that loud voice in your head telling you that you are crazy? Both these "parts" of the mind – survival and choice – are integral to us all but they oft times do not agree with each other.

When we act unconsciously, as we most often do, our self-images are given free reign to act out the expression of their particular worldview. The reason that this happens is the key to understanding the limitations that burden us. It is during our unconscious moments that we exhibit the behaviour that would often be deemed self-destructive, or in the least, not positive to our needs or safety. To look down and notice that you have eaten a whole cake by yourself while watching TV is but a mild representation of it. Few of us would look at a whole cake and say to ourselves:

"I'm going to eat this whole thing right now until I feel sick."

No, we usually realize after the fact that we have done the wrong thing, said the wrong thing, or rather, neglected to do the thing that we would have wanted to do. We do sometimes tell ourselves that we shouldn't be doing what we are doing, but we do it anyway, as if some puppet master was pulling our strings in spite of our protests.

We are left with the absurd situation whereby an extremely intelligent species lives a large portion of its life using only the most basic of its capacities, while the internally driven urge to spring forth and thrive is corked and placed in the cellar of our mind. Like a precious wine, it is left to age until some unknown glorious event graces us and we deem it worthwhile to take it out to the light to mark the celebration.

Our unconscious actions are our least common denominator and render us automatic in our responses to the stimulus that hits us. A basic plant is capable of such reaction. It, however, is capable of no more, while our responses are virtually limitless. To live in the "vegetative" state when there is so much more to life can certainly evoke in us a sense of the lost self. It is upon this, then, that we will address and shed light. We will let the eagle in us soar to the heights and leave the turnips in the field.

3

The Congo Line

In order to show that our many varied and contradictory views of our selves have come our way honestly, let's get a handle on the process the mind has undergone to get us where we are today. This, then, is the layperson's guide to the evolution of the mind, stated in one chapter! It's a little like the Minute Waltz performed in 5 seconds, but it certainly is enough for us to grasp how and why we see things the way we do. From layman to layman then, here is the view culled from exposure to that faculty called reasoning.

I have attempted to simplify this as much as possible, but this chapter does go into some basic principles of the brain's development. It won't be technical, but I need to demonstrate how things were a long time ago so that we can understand what is happening now. Stick with it; it will be worthwhile in the end.

The purpose here is to stop thinking that people have only one brain. We don't. We have some very old primitive parts up there working alongside the new stuff. As you will see, they don't quite know how to talk to each other, and we are stuck with the consequences.

As we journey back and look at our early ancestors before we became Homo Sapiens Sapiens (fully self-aware human, arguably around 150,000 years ago), let us try to imagine their worldview and the conditions, as they would have existed in those days.

We find the brain operated very differently than it does today. Our brains have evolved considerably since then, but the seeds to our wild and wacky ways were planted long before we had language, the wheel, or even CNN! So let us visit our ancestors in middle Africa.

The life expectancy of people at this time was not that great. It has been suggested that for the most part of human existence the average life expectancy was around 18 years. Humans are tribal creatures, like our primate cousins, and the survival of the tribe was paramount, so activities were, by nature, to that end. Therefore the race of humans banded together to find food, keep warm and dry, and avoid being eaten.

The ability to learn quickly the difference between danger and safety is a major survival tool for humans. Today we can see babies reaching out to put their hands into the mouths of strange dogs and running out into traffic without the slightest hint of instinct being present to forewarn the child. We know, therefore, that these reactions are not instinctive to us and must be learned.

So it was that our relationship with the environment was learned by observation and training by the adults. What to eat and drink, how to run and hide, what to hide from – all of these behaviours were learned early by the young individual. The actual length of adolescence in humans is significantly greater than that of other animals and attests to the amount of learning required by the individual in order to be a successful adult.

What we are interested in here, and how it applies to us, is the process by which the individual learns its relationship with the environment. We need to understand this process and have a language for it so that we can refer it forward to our present behaviour.

Please be conscious that we are still talking about the brain of our early ancestors, and although we have evolved other capacities since then, the process described here was the process available to them at the time. It is important to realize that when we don't use our new choices, these old ones are still in our brain and will automatically kick in and take over! This is actually the first clue to the enigma of our tug-of-war ways.

After The Batteries Are Inserted

Let's look at that moment that occurs sometime after the fertilized human egg has been dividing and specializing. Specifically, let's check the brain where upon being assembled, the batteries inserted, the switch is turned on and it immediately starts to do something.

The first thing that happens the moment the mind turns on is that it starts collecting data. All the senses start to feed this tiny brain data on every stimulus that befalls it. Every sense organ in the first weeks of life feeds the mind with millions of bits of data. Realize that every square millimetre of skin contains hundreds of sensors for pressure, pain, temperature, etc., so the quantity of data from all senses is almost hard to fathom.

It is very difficult for us to imagine the incredible capacity of the mind to collect data, simply because our senses don't bother informing us of the vast majority of the data coming in to them. If we could consciously list everything that the senses take in, in but one second of time, it would take days to list it all. Everything from: touch, taste, heat, colour, movement, rate of movement, dimension, volume, size, weight, texture, humidity, density, and on and on, all hitting this incredible mind every second of every day.

Just collecting data from the senses about the environment around us would not be enough to form meaning to the mind, just as knowing the letters of an alphabet does not give us language. The mind must have the ability to do something with these data. What it does, then, is compare all the information it receives with every other bit of information, and then compare each bit of this information to every other bit!

The amount of work done by the mind here is far beyond our capacity to conceive. This process, of course, is automatic and we do nothing consciously to help or hinder it.

This automatic process then proceeds to another capacity of the mind, and that is the ability to draw conclusions. After a while, the mind starts to see many similarities in the data coming in. Even though the amount of data entering the senses doesn't change, a lot of it is the same data as before. For example, all trees we see have leaves on them, even though they can be different in shape and colour. The smaller ones look the same as the big ones, and differ primarily in size.

After seeing enough of this relative sameness, an individual could go to another land where there is a very different species of tree and the mind would automatically know that this thing, which it has never seen before, is a tree. It is important to remember that this is a non-judgmental act. The mind simply notes, and has recognition of similarities. (Stay with me, there's hot chocolate and cookies at the end.)

17

When the mind needs to access the concept of "tree" because it sees one or thinks of one, these conclusions give the mind the capacity to access this information quickly. The speed of retrieval can be quite important, obviously. Wondering whether something is dangerous would not be an option. In a dangerous situation, we witness quick action indistinguishable from instinct. Humans, as well as the other animals, rely on this capacity to act without having to think first. Think of the lightning-fast process that removes our hand from a burning flame, even before we know that our hand is in the flame. It would be unwise to leave such decisions up to the part of the mind that would first have to notice the situation, contemplate an action, and then take the action. Survival events then would not be up for discussion.

What we have just described is the creation of an elaborate filing system. Imagine a computer screen with an icon for each file. The files contain all of the comparisons relative to data the computer is comparing. Visually, this label, or icon, would have an image attached to it, as well as instructions for how the file would initiate specific responses from the individual when the situation arose whereby the file would need to be accessed.

We will not spend too much time in this mind exploration, but it is very important to understand this very mechanical system because it is the creator of the person on the other end of the rope in the tug-of-war scenario called life. It shows up two very important points that we would do well to remember:

This all happens automatically.

There is no judgment whatsoever. None of these "conclusions" says good/bad or right/wrong.

A system whereby actions are initiated based on the filed data requires some sort of name for us to use. The unforgivable name, "Self Referencing Guidance System" (SRGS) is a big and horrible title but it evokes a very mechanical image, which is precisely what it is. It tells us, as we've said before, that all information that comes into the mind is automatically recorded and compared to everything else. Let us call it "The Protector", because that is the best description of its function.

Once a conclusion is reached about a category of, let's say – lion, all lions are referenced to the image in the mind. We are now triggered to actions based on what that conclusion tells us. If we wish to simplify the process so that we could visually comprehend it, it might look like this:

Imagine a man walking along the savannah when all of a sudden he sees a lion. The mind would "click" on the icon labelled "lion", which would contain all the pertinent instructions for his behaviour response written in it. Very crudely, the following flow chart would depict the process:

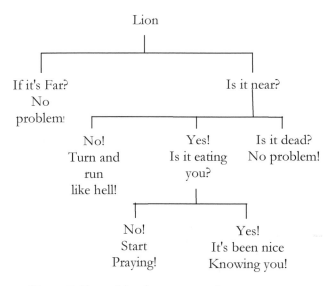

Figure 1: Everything is seen as an icon

It is important to remember that the system is self-referencing. The reason for this is that because everything is seen in relation to us, then who we are, according to the Self Referencing Guidance System (SRGS), is a relationship to all the things that we are not! Confusing? Look at it this way. When we see a tree, the mind has a file with a label on it called "tree". In that file, everything about trees and their consequent relationship to us is recorded. If we could talk to The Protector directly and ask it, "How tough is the human skin?" it could only reply, "Compared to what?" In the tree file, the human skin is less tough. Therefore The Protector knows that if we rub too hard against the tree, our skin will be damaged, not the tree. If we compare our skin

19

to water, then depending on the temperature (ice, slush, boiling, etc.) quantity, location on the body, (in the lungs, on the arm…), we get a different answer. That is what I mean by self-referencing. This part of the brain knows about us only by comparison of what everything else is in relation to itself.

This manner of analyzing input reflects other ways in which the brain functions. It is mirrored in our daily life when talking, thinking, or feeling about our self. Therefore, The Protector learns about what we are by what we are not!

Eh?

Hold on, it's coming.

The point is that The Protector is seeing us only in our relationship to the environment. This is the first process called a self-image. To The Protector, self-image is only a comparison of us to the outside world. Our behaviour for each situation up to this point in our development is automatically tied to the self-image associated with it. See a lion – run like hell, hungry – eat, etc. For primitive humans that caused no problems, and in fact was exactly what kept them alive. They were not about to jump over a cliff on a whim or try to mate with a gorilla. They wouldn't even find a gorilla attractive enough because the automatic injunctions learned about getting near a very powerful creature such as this would keep them from such suicidal contemplations.

The Protector was the system for survival and we can be sure that it had measures to ensure that nothing would interfere with its ability to cause the individual to act. For us today, it is a very different story, as we will see. Remember that this system still operates in us today, although it is no longer alone. Back then, it was the guidance system. So let us remember these statements for now because we will see the consequences of them later. The Protector is always seeing us in relation to the world outside.

The automatic conclusions resulting from the comparing of all the data our mind receives and compares, produces one of the elements that we today call self-images. These are automatically created and are only a comparison of the individual to everything else.

The self-images dictate the dominant behaviour of primitive humans and most animals in any given situation.

THE CONGO LINE

The self-images described here are simply the conclusions of The Protector and not the sense of self you have the ability to develop today!

Let us remember the period by which all of this has been prefaced. We are looking at the evolution of the mind and the development of thinking and awareness. Humankind has qualities much like his primate kin at this time and is not yet fully self-aware. The capacity for self-awareness that separated us from the other animals has not yet appeared. The process of creating self-image is still the same processes that others animals have.

Don't imbue the term self-image with the connotation of emotion and judgment that it has today. It was literally the result of the summaries by the mind as it saw, felt, tasted, touched, and heard the world around it. That is why up to this time the term "Self Referencing Guidance System" was used to give you an image of it as a mechanical result rather than a judgmental one. In addition, because most animals have brains that do the same thing to a certain degree, we should reserve the term self-image for the next stage of humankind, when she or he could really dictate a concept of self.

The Self Referencing Guidance System and self-image up to this time is the same thing. Our ancestors would never call it a self-image. They couldn't, because the idea of self was not developed. Just as a cat can have a calm personality, the cat doesn't know it has a calm personality. The cat doesn't even know his tail is a part of "it".

The important thing to realize, and to keep conscious of, is that the creation of these self-references were an automatic process of the mind, and that this process is essentially the same for most animals.

At some point in time and by some wonderful process that probably took thousands of years, humans became self-aware creatures. How and when this happened does not matter for the sake of our discussion here. What is important is that we understand that the quality of self-awareness is the quality of knowing that we know. We not only think, but we know that we think. We can think about thinking. Furthermore, self-awareness allows us to conceptualize things that are not there yet nor invented.

Whenever self-awareness "kicked in", these later people were now aware that they were learning new things, and could actually conceptualize how things out there related to them.

It is difficult to fathom this period of our development because we have progressed quite far from there, but try to imagine the leap from people not knowing that they had a personality, to actually being able to imagine the possibility of changing it! Before this, an individual could love; now they knew they were in love and could contemplate the concept of love. Love, or any other emotion, was now a thing, something that one can talk about, whereas before, it happened without conscious thought.

The Protector was no longer hidden from the consciousness of humankind. Conclusions drawn from the comparing of all the data coming in could be sensed as a change in "personality." One would still not try to mate with a gorilla, but now we knew we were crazy even to bring up the idea! It was a monumental time for humankind. It was the true beginning of that system called the self-image. It was still automatic and happened without our help, but for the most part, people were now aware of these self-images.

The onset of self-awareness had very positive repercussions for us, but it created problems as well. Before self-awareness, humankind was, in a sense, taken care of by nature or the gods, if you will. Like the beasts that roamed the forests and plains, they had the ability to learn how to create complex tools, count higher than two, and conceptualize things that were not in front of them.

The young lion cub is taught by its mother to hunt, and then matures and hunts without thinking about it. It is, in a sense, looked after by the gods. The gods in this way also protected humans.

With the advent of self-awareness, humans actually had the ability to think beyond the conclusions of their mechanical mind. Their musings about how things were actually became new data that, because of the way we know The Protector works, formed new conclusions. This was the first time in our history that conclusions or self-images could be created by data created by consciousness or ego. Before, everything was a conclusion based on external data; now data could be created from a new source – internal contemplation.

THE CONGO LINE

Up to this point in time, there was nothing in humankind's mental development to cause excessive problems. Our old friend, The Protector, was continuously improving our ability to function and survive. It was the great protector. We see in countless animals the extent to which their developments have brought them in regards to survival. Defence mechanisms and offensive mechanisms keep species alive.

People were, and still are, part of this system. This function obviously holds a high priority to the mind. Now our new self-awareness challenges all that. From the point of view of the self-images, the greatest threat to The Protector has just been created!

4

Genesis

Visualize a colour-blind woman whose world comprises shades of grey. Imagine the beauty missed. The satin splash of a red rose, the calming vista of a verdant field, the crayon box array of a cosmopolitan streetscape, or the blue-green twinkle in a child's eyes. Picture her living without this splendour for thirty years when, one day, due to some sort of accident, or magic wish, her colour sight is fully restored.

In but a moment, a flood of information comes into her unsuspecting mind as, second after second, everything that was known, safe, predictable, and intimate, transforms into a further dimension before her eyes. As the common becomes the transmuted, her mind not only has to contend with the addition of colour in of itself, but even more so, the intertwining of emotions triggered by the effect of the colours on her psyche. The objects previously known, which before had a certain charm or beauty, now evoke in her, feelings whose depths were hitherto unknown. Colour itself now becomes an option in selecting one item over another. It now becomes a new parameter in the palette of choice.

There would be an astonishing adjustment period as her mind processed this newfound standard, one that would have a major impact as to how she would gauge her world.

If we can absorb the magnitude of change incited by the addition of a "quality" of just one sense, as colour was to sight in the example just given, then ponder the epiphany as humans went from an incredible but unconscious adaptive species, to a self-aware conceptual creator! This metamorphosis in human evolution, this non-celestial big bang, came to humans as a great conqueror invades a land. It usurped the ruling dictator, the unconscious reflexive mandarin of action/reaction – The Protector relegated it to a lower position and sat in its place as an inquisitive and ponderous ruler called The Will.

Let's take a breath and climb down from the rarefied atmosphere of metaphor for a moment to paint this picture in plain English. The enormity of this event or process is so fundamental to the understanding of our greatness, as well as to the source of our problems, that words wax poetic in tribute to the event. If we can capture this idea in our minds, then we will have the power it contains laid triumphantly at our feet!

This pivotal point in our history was so long ago and it took a long time to develop, yet if we look at our mythology, we can see that its importance did not escape our unconscious need to acknowledge its inception. In the Bible, in Genesis, we find the verse:

"Both were naked, the man and the wife, but they had no feeling of shame." Gen. 2:25

Then, because Adam and Eve ate the forbidden fruit, it goes on to say:

"Then the eyes of both of them were opened, and they knew that they were naked; so they stitched fig-leaves together and made themselves loincloths." Gen. 3:7

These quite revealing passages are not saying that our biblical parents walked around with their eyes closed, nor is it saying that they were so stupid that Adam, who, it was written, named all the animals and trees, couldn't figure out that he was naked! No, what we have here is the mythological representation of the moment that we became self-aware. Consciousness of shame, or indeed any reflective opinion, can only happen with self-awareness. The eating of the forbidden fruit was the metaphor for its inception.

When God confronts Adam, who was hiding in the garden, Adam says:

"…I was afraid because I was naked, so I hid."

God then asks, "Who told you that you were naked? Have you eaten from the tree that I forbade you to eat from?" Gen. 3:11

The eating of the forbidden fruit gave Adam the knowledge of his own nakedness. God knew that Adam had eaten of the fruit because his answer to God was a self-aware statement. His language now contained references back to self, which was a sure giveaway.

Within the framework of the myth, we witness the perfect setup. Let's recap the events. We have an infallible god creating two people by using absolute power. Then, this same god creates a beautiful garden full of trees of all kinds, and then tells his protégés that they can eat whatever fruit they want, just not from these two trees! These trees, we will remember happen to be contain the fruit of our human downfall. I presume that there was no other safe place to put these trees. If I follow this legend correctly, God gives them these instructions and then leaves them alone. We are then to believe that God, the creator of this primordial pair, didn't know what was going to happen. I try to picture God coming back from wherever an omniscient being could go, and saying, "Oh my me, what have you done"? We are left to believe either that God, in creating his first park, didn't know about playground safety, or that the whole thing was a setup to get them to do exactly what he knew they would do.

What we have in the beautiful, if not clumsy Genesis story, is a tale depicting a loving parent getting the kids out of the house at the right time, but giving them the tools for personal responsibility. Crafty parenting! This is not a story about free choice. Rather, we have the mythological representation of the moment when we became self-aware. God fledged us from the house so we could fend for our selves. All other animals remained the "trustees" of God. The "fruit" of the trees, were the tools to do it.

The tree was not the tree of everyday knowledge, but specifically the tree of self-knowledge. The serpent told them that they would be like gods with the power to create, and indeed that is what happened. Verse 22 of Chapter 3 quotes God as saying:

"The man had become like one of us, knowing good and evil..."

This knowing right from wrong was obviously viewed as a criteria for god-hood and indicated that humankind had been elevated above all the other animals in the kingdom, insofar the ability to conceptualize and create. Let us make sure that we all understand that when Adam and Eve "knew' evil", it was not the ability to point out and say – "Ah there it is. I never noticed it before."

Evil is not out there in nature. All animals live according to their design and are not wilfully malicious, just as a hurricane isn't out to get us. When Adam and Eve ate the fruit, they gained a capacity to create the concept of right and wrong. Self-awareness brings with it the ability to conceptualize a new reference point that is centered on the self.

With the creation of "I", came the extension "us." The "us" had to have its reflection, and so there was, in the same instant, the creation of "them."

The Hebrew God had a vengeful personality. The Old Testament texts are full of images of a god with quite the temper. He certainly had the concept of "us and them", and when "they" ticked him off, he was not above wiping out the whole village in revenge. This is perhaps why the god in Genesis said that..."man had become like one of us." Gen. 3:22

Self-awareness changed our relationship with nature forever. Before self-awareness, humans were an integral part of nature. Now they were raised above it in the sense of being able to create a world of their design. They could conceptualize a home and build it rather than stumbling about in the elements until they found a natural shelter.

Our word for nature, "environment", derived from Middle English and the French, "environs", means, "That which surrounds the viewer." The implication of the word is that the environment is around us, not that we are a part of it, and therefore puts us at the center of it. Thus, even when we speak of the environment, we are unconsciously excluding ourselves from it. That may go a long way in explaining the state of the environment today.

The rest of the animals and plants had natural laws to ensure their existence; humans could now ensure their own! The automatic processes that the mind had developed were now in competition for control of the actions and reactions of the individuals in their care. They could not be easily annulled, as we will see they still are very much present most of the time, but they were now no longer, strictly speaking, in charge!

The methods employed by The Protector to keep individuals alive and safe were about to get very complicated. The new Will character was not there to help The Protector. It blatantly caused individuals to do things that the self-images in the past would have kept them from doing. How could these two systems get along? The Will certainly had dominance over our self-images, as it does today, but the old self-images are so powerful it sometimes takes great emotional strength to go against their dictates. Of course, if we remember that our self-images were created and treated as a survival tool, we can well understand that any attempt to change any self-image is seen as a threat to the self.

Millions of years of evolution prepared The Protector for defence against this new Will character, and even though The Will is more powerful, the self-images still have many ways of exerting their influence, always with the goal of protecting the self-image (and only by extension, the individual) who is being threatened. In addition, it must be pointed out that, even though The Will is the great commander, and its creation changed all the rules that governed us up to this time, The Will is a fickle ruler. Most of the time, our Will leaves the governing of the state, our daily life, up to the self-images.

Thus, we have the situation that is prevalent today, whereby there is a battle between our self-images and our Will. One is the great protector, the other the great freedom fighter; the former, a hard-wired program, the latter, a moment-by-moment sense of direction that springs from the true emerging self.

We can now emphasize the points that make clear the dichotomy of our duelling minds:

The nature of our self-images is to protect themselves in order to protect their learned version of us.

The nature of The Will is to seek fulfillment of the desires and dreams that inspire us.

5

The Battle Begins

The driving force behind evolution is the advancement of a species towards a greater perfection, defined by the success of the survivorship of the species. We see some animals, such as the shark, in which evolutionary advancement has reached such a level that fossil records indicate that they have changed little over millions of years.

Humans have a variety of these amazing adaptive traits. In the cold arctic, the people have flat noses and stubby fingers, which, because of the diminished surface area, retain more heat. In the hottest areas of the globe, people have developed dark to black skin to keep from burning. Some became tall, with long fingers and limbs, which dissipate heat readily.

The proof of our success as a species is all around us. We have learned to live in every climatic condition of the world. We have tamed rivers and mountains, lakes and deserts like no other animal on this earth.

For now, let us keep certain obvious facts out of the discussion, such as pollution of our air and water, chemicals in our foods, and the long list of things we have done that seemingly leads us down the road to self-destruction. That is a later discussion. Barring all of this, we are nature's proud pet project. We need to see the difference between nature's design for us, and our intervention on nature's design. If we look strictly at humankind's evolutionary traits, that is, nature without a second opinion from us, we have unquestionably adapted to our world with an amazing level of proficiency.

Does it not seem likely that, as with other animals, nature would want to protect the systems, processes and traits that made us this way? Natural selection would weed out the traits that are less useful, and keep the ones that ensure the success of the species. This is as true with humans as it is with other species. In the case of humans, The Protector would have developed a system to ensure itself that it is guarded from tampering.

"THROUGH THE DOOR!"

Here we come to the next key point in our understanding of how all of this affects us today. The mind, in its evolutionary development, would most assuredly see this basic feature of itself to draw conclusions from data, that is, to create self-images, as one of the vital features needing protection.

Because so often in the life of pre-self-aware humans, timing speed and quick reflexes were so essential to the survival of the species, the mind could not afford to have the individual tamper consciously with these self-images.

Just think of the consequences of a curious individual walking up to a hungry lion and saying hello! These created self-images that identify the relationship the individual has to the environment, would most surely require a mechanism to make it tamper proof from the whim of choice.

There was no problem as long as a human wasn't self-aware. In the animal world, whenever a predator is in the observable vicinity, animals get frightened. The animal responds to the fear and this causes the appropriate reaction. They cannot change their mind and decide to communicate a message of peace to the predator.

In essence then, the lack of self-awareness is actually a part of the mechanism that helps ensure the safety of animals, including non-self-aware humankind.

The self-image establishes the relationship and behaviour to the predator. The lack of self-awareness ensures that animals will essentially react the same predictable way to the predator every time. This does not negate curiosity, which many animals exhibit, but animal curiosity doesn't violate the basic traits of survivorship.

Once they learn a fear of something, and a self-image relating to that thing is created, curiosity will rarely violate that self-image.

The advent of self-awareness changed all that in humans. We were no longer in the Garden of Eden. We knew pain, fear, shame, embarrassment, death and dying. Humans became the only creature who could seemingly contemplate death. (It is possible that elephants will do this also). Additionally, we could now contemplate life. The problem with this is that along with contemplation comes curiosity.

THE BATTLE BEGINS

Self-awareness gave the new humans desires. It also brought them the need to find answers to those things that produced fear but were themselves intangible. Lightning, thunder, eclipses, love, hate, death – these things could be heard or felt but could not be held.

The mind on its own would come to conclusions, but consciousness could find no easy answers. The Will or conscious self now had a need to understand and rationalize that which it could not totally grasp. The need to know was simply created by the new capacity of the aware mind to see cause and effect in a conceptual way.

That is the nature of our ability to invent. To invent, whether it is a thing, a myth, or a theory, one needs be able to visualize a cause or problem and then consider the effect or solution.

This is not the process involved with animals that we see using tools. In their case, the problem is not conceptual but tangible and needs not result from the "what if/then" process which is present in any problem-solving situation. That was fancy jargon just to say that there is a big difference between using a stick to get ants out of a hole, and making an axe to chop wood. (It must be said that this point of view is being challenged by new information that is suggesting that some animals are seemingly displaying some rather advanced thinking that may suggest more awareness than previously thought. It doesn't change what we are saying about human capacities and may even function to knock our egos down to a more realistic level.)

Self-reflective thought was in itself a tool, and now humans could use it to tamper with their own self-images. This was the beginning of our salvation, and our problems! The old self-images in self-aware humans still have all of their features existing from their beginnings as a survival process. They still are a result of comparing everything they absorb through the senses. They still do so automatically. They still have built-in protective devices that keep unaware humans from harm. They still are indistinguishable from instinct in their ability to create automatic behaviours in us when we are not conscious of our actions.

We have spoken as to how humans are tribal. We survived and thrived because of our ability to work together, hunt together, and cooperate. Without this cooperative tribal capacity, it is doubtful that our clawless, naked, slow forbearers would have survived. Therefore,

The Protector had to conclude that tribal behaviour led to survival, and non-tribal behaviour led to death. Therefore, humans had the tendency to fear straying far from the tribe, both physically and developmentally.

This behaviour contrasted sharply from the desires of The Will. It desired to seek adventure, to risk to achieve an end, even the act of being different, all of which translated to stepping outside the boundaries of the tribe. This, like the other qualities of The Will, came in direct conflict with the self-image system that had the simple mandate of survival. It would seem that these two systems vied against each other because they threatened each other's desired outcomes.

In the early stages of aware humans, most of the self-images were still created because of our interaction with nature. Now The Protector had to contend with The Will's sometimes-flagrant disregard for the perceived dangers. The Will, on the other hand, had to contend with the ever-vigilant Protector, which executed its influence on the individual whenever an unconscious moment presented itself.

The creation of The Will would forever change the nature of the reality of the individual, and therefore the tribes. The mind was to witness an influx of data from a source that had never existed before, that of the conceptual construct, and in so doing, create a whole series of conflicting self-images.

Humans, in their new conscious capacity, were becoming dabblers of self-images. At first, there was only the relationship with the environment.

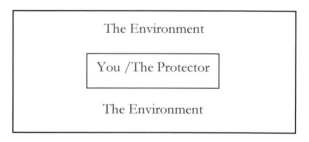

Figure 2: You and the environment

THE BATTLE BEGINS

With the advent of self-awareness came the awareness of – "me" or "I". I could choose to do things that The Protector would have had complete control over before. Now there were two opponents and the game of tug of war began.

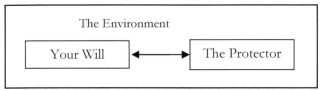

Figure 3: The Will enters the playground

Whenever an individual even contemplated the idea of, say, taking food away from a feasting lion, The Protector simply instilled a tremendous sense of fear and the individual changed the subject. There were times; however, when, in spite of The Protector's attempts at control, an individual would manage to overcome the fear and proceed against the fear. Something such as climbing a high tree to get fruit was now possible because someone acted in spite of the fear triggered by The Protector.

The environment from the point of view of The Protector included everything that was not the individual. Therefore, even the tribe was seen as part of the environment.

Before self-awareness, there was the law of the jungle, but now humans started to create a few laws of their own. They had a tool in their arsenal that no other species had – that of a fully reflective language. These laws, rules, dictates and opinions were not in direct response to nature. These were lofty inferences, created in the minds of individuals in an attempt to understand and explain the unknown, and then passed on to their tribes as fact.

These facts were treated by the self-image system as all other data must be treated – compared to all other data and a conclusion drawn as to their relevance to survival! We all know what this translated to on the broad tribal level. Gods, religions, rituals, superstitions, human sacrifices and war were just a few of the tribal consequences of the mind's rationale. So, on the other hand, were pottery, poetry, agriculture, laws and music.

The weakness of The Will lay in the fact that it is something to be evoked. For so many thousands of years, humans relied on the The Protector to protect them.

The Protector had an incredibly brilliant system to ensure the status quo, and at the same time sneak by The Will and rule the individual for the major part of his and her life. When we look at people's behaviours today, we can readily see this flip-flop of action/inaction, two steps forward – one step back, consequence of The Will and self-images taking their turn at driving the bus!

Abraham Maslow (1954) developed the concept of the "Hierarchy of Needs" to explain the path of individual evolution as a person develops his or her own sense of self. It is by now a very familiar concept, but as a refresher for you, it states that individuals follow a prescribed path of needs fulfillment whereby the first step must be satisfied before the individual can contemplate the next one. At the base of his hierarchy of needs is the need to survive. Maslow states that the individual must sense that survival is not in question before moving forward to other pursuits. Once this level is achieved, one can allow one's resources to focus on the next level, which is security. The progression is to belonging, self-esteem and self-actualizing.

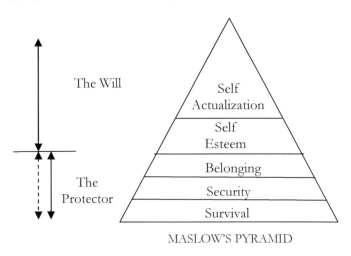

MASLOW'S PYRAMID

Figure 4: Maslow (1954), in relation to The Will

THE BATTLE BEGINS

If you look at this progression, you can see the reflection of the tug-of-war as it plays out. The SRGS or Protector is first concerned with the survival, security, and sense of belonging of the individual and the tribe. It is the most primitive of drives in humans.

Once past belonging, you enter into realms that are very much a representation of humans with our self-aware abilities. To seek self-esteem, one must be aware of the self. We can further state that primarily The Protector directs the lower end of Maslow's pyramid, while the upper half is the domain of The Will. Do note that The Will also dabbles in the lower realms, for free choice is just that – the freedom to be poor if you want to, the freedom to be alone. Now most of the time when people in a developed country are not satisfied, the reason is usually temporary, situational, or the third player in our game of self. That we will get into later!

The first two players in the tug-of-war of our life are now visible. In this corner – The Protector, with its scripted, automatic, non-judgmental system; in the other corner – The Will with its free-reign curiosity.

Sometimes they both want to go in the same direction and our life seems smooth and automatic…then, there is the rest of our life!

I have said that The Protector is non-judgmental and that its automatic processes are based on the conclusions it has drawn. This does not explain why then you "feel" so conflicted sometimes, or stupid, shy, defeated etc.

If there is no judgment, why then are we so judgmental? Alas, therein lies the tale! I said that The Protector was non-judgmental; I did not say that it was stupid. It had millions of years to develop and during this time, certainly learned a few tricks to ensure the survival of the individual. When The Will came along, it was ready to go into action to fight The Protector. The result of this we feel today.

The Protector learned the great art of hiding right in front of our eyes. Even now as we point to it, The Protector will fight us, and try to hide. From now on, pay close attention to the changes in how you feel as you read on.

The Protector is listening. It is starting to suspect that something is up. It is going to try to stop you from continuing. The difference between the people that "get" the point of the book, and those that don't, balances on this pivot. You have self-awareness, so pay attention to your feelings!

6

The Relationship Tag

We have just described the beginning of the tug-of-war between The Will and The Protector. The Protector has its ideas and we have a few ideas of our own. When you think about it, our daily life isn't often full of situations where we are facing life-and-death decisions. Of course, when we cross the road we do what is necessary not to be run over by traffic. When we are driving, we stay in our lane, stop at lights and keep vigilant of the actions of the other driver. Around the house, we don't lean on stove elements, and we don't pick up knives by the sharp end.

We do not spend much time thinking about all of these events that safety related. Oh sure, late at night when no one is around, we may go right through a stop sign or even a red light, but even there we do so when the risk is virtually non-existent. In other words, we are not in any real danger.

The Tug-of-war between our Will and The Protector is very rarely about those things that relate to the environment and us. Our emotional battles center on issues such as:

- Should I ask him/her out?
- Should I speak up and tell the truth?
- Do I take the new job?
- Do I quit my job that I hate so much?
- Can I really get away with wearing this?

Should I tell him what I really think?

These things cause you the most grief. The daily things that come into the category of:

- Should have
- Would have
- Could have
- If only…
- If it wasn't for…

These types of problems that plague most individuals have nothing to do with our relationship with the environment, or our relationship with our self. In all of the above statements, there is rarely anyone asking him or her self:

"What do I think?"

All of these "problems" have that famous tacit question behind them:

"What will they think?"

In other words, we create stress because the opinion of the tribe now comes into play. As we have outlined before, being in a tribe is the way we have survived as a species. The tribe has therefore been extremely important to us. Our language came about because the tribe needed it, not because individuals needed it.

We suffer more anguish, indecision and pain from how we think other people will think of us than any other cause. So much of our daily behaviour is automatically geared to behaving in a way that doesn't cause others to look at us disapprovingly. Most often, it is an automatic response to something that has happened to us in the past. What this means is that we are more often reliving and re-enacting historical events rather than living and being in the present

If we are humming to ourselves, waiting for the elevator, we usually stop when the doors open and there are people inside; not because we do not want to disturb them, but because we don't want them to think ill of us. We would not necessarily be aware of our motive for stopping, and we may not even be aware that we have stopped humming.

In Chapter One, we alluded to the fact that there were three separate processes that we group together and call self-images.

- Our relation to the environment.
- Our relation to our self.
- Our relation to the tribe.

We have now unveiled the third and most critical process, and that is that of our relationship to the tribe. In our tug-of-war analogy, we see that it actually is more complex than the simple two-sided game.

Instead of being the traditional two-directional pull-pull,

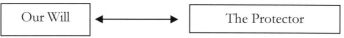

Figure 5: The basic "Tug of War"

THE RELATIONSHIP TAG

We have a three-way tug-of-war like this:

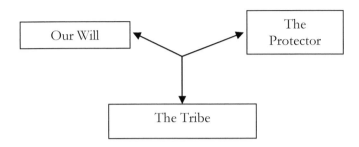

Figure 6: Three-way "Tug of War"

Here is an example of this three-pronged situation as it occurs in youth. Some young boys are on the roof of a garage and daring each other to jump to the ground. One boy is urged to go first. His Protector assesses the situation and decides that it is dangerous. It starts tightening its rope, producing legitimate fear in the boy who senses that the action is dangerous, so of course he hesitates.

The other boys start with:

"Come on ya big chicken!"

Now the other rope starts to tighten. This rope leads directly from the tribe, and pulls on the boy's self-image.

"What will they think if I don't?

They won't like me if I don't.

They'll think I'm a big baby!"

Alternately, the boy may come to the realization that he is always letting others tell him what to do and just because someone tells you that you're a chicken, doesn't mean that you have to listen.

It is at this point that the boy either jumps, because he is afraid of what the others will say if he doesn't, or he doesn't jump, because he is afraid of what will happen to him physically if he does, or he tells the others that they can do what they want, but he isn't interested. The outcome depends on what is stronger at the time, the fear of real danger, the tribal disfavour, or invoking The Will and making a self-driven decision.

"THROUGH THE DOOR!"

Occasionally, a youngster will have enough of a developed sense of self that is enough to be able to let his Will pull against these other two ropes. He may say something such as, "If you're so tough, you do it". He might even think to himself that the leader is always trying to get people to do things and simply refuse to do it, not out of fear, but rather because he simply has no need to blindly follow the crowd.

Really though, what happens most of the time? What force is evoked the most often? During grade school, high school and most of university or college, the strongest force seems to be undoubtedly, the force of the tribe. Very few individuals do not succumb to the peer pressure of fashion, jargon, and attitude, to be a part of the crowd. The majority of individuals who reject fashion will do so, not to reject the tribe, but to identify themselves as a member of another tribe – the rebels. It is still a tribal gesture.

By far, the majority of stress one feels on a daily basis stems from not wanting to incur the disfavour of the tribe. Virtually all advertisements use this fact to "encourage" us to purchase a product. They show situations where people will think we are:

- Stupid
- Smelly
- Unclean
- Poor
- Non-sexy
- Fat
- Too short
- Too tall
- Too old
- Too young
- Fill in the blanks

Companies spend hundreds of billions of dollars each year in advertisements around the world. Start paying attention to the ads you see on television with the questions in your mind:

"Who are they saying will be happy if I buy this product – me or them?"

"Does it tell me I'll be happy for my own sake, or because others will see me in a more favourable way?"

THE RELATIONSHIP TAG

We will see that most commercials have an effect on us precisely because they focus on what others will think. In other words, we are encouraged at every step of the way to change ourselves in order to be more loved, liked, and better thought of. You may in a moment of defiance say, "I don't care what they think!" More than likely, there is a different tribe that you care about than the casually referred to "they". Of course, some people do get past the tribe and this is the point of this book. The ability to wear an orange blouse with your red hair simply because you feel like it is a liberating feeling when you do not worry about what everyone else thinks of you. If you're bothering to read this, it is more likely though that there is a tribe out there exerting its influence on you.

Many people rebel against the ideas of the people around them. Street gangs are an extreme example of this. We can clearly see with the street gangs though, with their gang colours, common language and similar clothing, that they have merely joined another tribe. Nothing else has changed and the tribe is still the focus.

The question to ask ourselves is; whom am I trying to impress, or get a reaction from by my words and actions? We may get some small pleasure by being different for difference sake but that, unfortunately, still ties us to the tribe. We may have simply gotten to like the idea that says, "I'm different", and our motivation is based on the feelings that it gives us to be different.

To be different implies different from something, and that something is still the tribe. Hence, the desire to be not of the tribe still means that the focus is the tribe. What most of you are looking for and would like to be acquainted with are those desires, wishes, dreams and realities that are born in your own mind and not as a function of others. That is something else entirely.

Our world then revolves around the biological fact that the primate in us is compelled to be tribal. Regardless of our personal self-aware longings, we also have a very strong mechanism urging us to be at one with our tribe. The Protector , who never sleeps and always collects data, and then forms conclusions (as we've said enough times now), would conclude that anything that keeps the tribe together must be good for the individual, and therefore exerts a pressure on us to conform to the tribe's wishes.

It was a simple, straightforward process to conclude that a lion will kill us or not, or that a fall from a cliff will kill us or not. These conclusions we can agree with. But the information that The Protector was to gather from the communication by tribe members through words, tone-of-voice, or body language, had no real, tangible, or verifiable external measurement that The Protector could use to reach its conclusions. A fall from a tree is easy for The Protector to grasp, and consequently produce the proper response of caution in us as a means of protecting us. What can it do though with the tribe's new concept of stupidity, or ugliness? That information doesn't mean anything tangible from an environmental point of view, therefore its conclusions had to be based on the intensity of the information given. We will make the case later, but let us just say here that the information coming to our minds in the form of an opinion, or an intangible idea, is as real as a bite in the ass from a tiger!

This process then, this third end to the rope whereby the opinions of other pulls on our decisions, is what we can usefully call a "Relationship Tag". Although it feels like a self-image, its creation came about by our relation to others in the tribe. The closer they were to us, the closer the intensity of the Tag. In other words, a parent's view of you was the most important to you when you were a small child. Then as you grew, the opinion of your peers' started to weigh heavier as your tribes began to encompass more people.

Understanding the Relationship Tag

To understand how this all works, let's look at your young, innocent, and fertile child mind. A child's mind is a voracious learning machine. It is said that you learn more in the first few years of life than in the rest of the years that follow. There is so much that is different from one day to the other. As a child, you live in "sponge mode", absorbing everything that is going on around you. Adults who are the source of much of your first knowledge, and exalted to the position of "The Omnipotent Ones" by your hungry little mind, often seem determined, even if it is not intentional, to teach you not only the nature of the world, but to define your nature as well. They do this most often by defining you, not unto yourself, but as a relationship to them, the adult.

Where the adult "came from" had a major bearing on what you, as a child, saw in yourself when they interacted with you. The labels you created related more to the feelings triggered in you by the adults, and what they saw in you moment by moment, based on their worldview. Very little of it was related to the actual qualities that you possess.

These labels, or Relationship Tags, became the majority of those things that today you identify as your self-image. They are also clearly different from self-images formed by your relationship with the environment. These images were ideas others imparted on you. By strict definition, they should not be called self-images, because the person who initiated them was not "your self".

Therefore, the Self Referencing Guidance System or The Protector creates our relation to the environment. The Relationship Tags are created by our relationship to the "tribe" (or the individuals that make up our circle of influence.

Look at these two examples. If you want, you can believe that they are an exaggeration or caricature of people rather than a reality that happens far too often.

Picture a very inquisitive young child, one that very naturally asks a multitude of questions. Imagine a set of parents wrapped up with their own personal lives to the point that their threshold for attending to the needs of the youngster is very low. See those times when even before the child opened his mouth, they tell him to be quiet, or go play, or find anything else to do but be around the parent.

Let us now contrast this story with another one, whereby we have the same child but a different set of parents. Let's make these parents the "model" kind who see their little one as a gift, and work toward nurturing the individuality of their child.

As this child starts asking the same excess of questions, we see one parent or the other opening up picture books to show the why and wherefore of things, and interacting positively to their little one's questions. As the parents become tired, as we all become eventually, we see the parents declining to answer all the questions. Not with a discursive gesture, or the implication that the child is a pest, but reinforcing that, although the question is brilliant, and the child is obviously bright for asking it, it will still have to wait for another time for the response that certainly will be forthcoming.

We need not be Freud to see that the two scenarios would provide the child with very different data with which his mind would form quite different conclusions about the self. The information the mind ingests as facts, are the ideas, opinions, and beliefs of the parents. This is not the same as tangible responses to constants found in nature.

The first set of parents in these scenarios would create a different foundation in the individual then the second set. This seems to be true and our experience and observation seems to support it. We know, as an example, from studies that children from abusive families are predisposed to grow up and become abusers themselves.

The problem with what we know and what our experience seems to show us is that this whole scenario involves that ancient and survival-specific part of the brain, The Protector, which now incorporated intangible information from outside and naturally treated it as real information.

Our "pre-Eden" brain functioned in a manner quite different than it does today. Its role of Protector was to take all the tangible information it could take in and from this, form conclusions that induced us to take appropriate action. This early computer now had to treat all of these tribal concepts in the same way because that is what it was programmed to do! However, the results of the "data" cannot be properly called a self-image.

If we take the term self-image in its most literal sense, then a self-image is the way we see ourselves. It is our view of us, not someone's suggestion, or influence, but our view of self. If we could ask our Will, "Who are you?" and it could answer purely, without the background chorus of self-image's questions, it would say:

"I am…"

The answer would have to be in the present tense. Who you are is just that; who you are. It is not a function of who you were, or who you will be. To the Will, you are not anywhere else but here now.

46

THE RELATIONSHIP TAG

Anything else is just a label or a Tag. In fact, all these labels or Tags affixed to us are nothing more than Relationship Tags. They are but a reflection of our relationship to others. This term states the position quite clearly, and we can envision a label stuck to our forehead called "shy", "clumsy", "stupid", or any of a profusion of Tags available to those who lent their perception of who they saw when they looked at us.

A self-image would be something we see in ourselves, a true quality that comes from that part of ourselves which makes us truly different from others. These other things called Relationship Tags act on the assumption that they define us and so they constantly attempt to dictate our behaviour.

When we were young, we were tagged with qualities (which we then accepted as ours) based upon the feelings or beliefs of those who related to us. It is a stunning revelation that we are filled with Tags that represent those relationships with others mixed in with the qualities that are genuinely ours.

These Relationship Tags are not based in any kind of reality that has anything to do with us. To The Protector, though, they are as real as the self-image that says, "I am not to walk out directly into the path of a moving car", and so The Protector treats them as something vital to protect.

Is it possible that a child can reject the ideas of the parents? Cannot a young child exercise her Will and just say to herself that the parent is wrong? Have you ever heard of a young child of parents of any orthodox religion deciding to become an atheist? The rise of fundamentalism all over the world is an example of parents reinforcing their ideas upon their children. The fervour by which this occurs is producing children with such narrow points of view that it is very difficult to open a dialogue with them on any other possibilities. Such is the strength of the Relationship Tag.

I was born and raised in Toronto, Ontario. My father was a French Canadian from Quebec and consequently a die-hard Montreal Canadiens fan. It never occurred to me as a youngster that while I cheered for the Montreal Canadiens too, the Toronto Maple Leafs was more a representation of the tribe where I was born and was living. I cheered for a team in another city far away, simply because that is what my father did and I automatically followed suit. In other words, my dad's tribe was my de facto tribe.

Very young children have a strong need for acceptance and approval. If and how that approval is given produces the first and most influential Tags that will govern the way a child grows up. The very young child has a built-in sense of knowing where its survival depends. Maslow's pyramid would suggest that the survival mode is in high gear here. Everything from the smell of the child, to the defenceless sound of its cries, stirs in us deep feelings of protectiveness for the infant.

Survival matters more than anything does at first. While children are learning survival skills, The Will is developing, and exercising itself. That is one reason for little children to be defiant, shouting "no" every two minutes to the parents. The other reason has to do with learning the cause and effect of language. Nevertheless, the more primitive part of our brain that deals with survival runs the show until we reach a certain level of maturity.

What is sure is that, to the little people, the giants called parents bring food, shelter, clothing and comfort. This gives parents a tremendous influence over their children. When we say parents here, let us be sure that we know that it is not just to the biological parents that we refer. Extended family members, older siblings, teachers, and any person in the position of apparent authority have the weight of influence on the child. In our western world, the circle of influence for our children is usually contained in a small circle of parents, teachers, the day-care worker, plus the great equalizers of them all, television and the internet!

Most primates live in troupes or tribes because they can survive better, and their very social nature makes the troupe an ideal system. As primates ourselves, we humans differ little from our chimp and ape relatives in this nature. We may be more complex in the make-up of our tribes, but we live in them, nonetheless. The troupes' survival is favoured over that of the individual. The very concept of a Bill of Human Rights is so new in our human history. It is amazing that this act of standing up for the individual survived to become a principle in the few countries where it exists. We know in practice that this is an ideal fought for, but at any moment can be taken away if the tribe feels threatened by the gesture. In the U.S.A., we have seen States give the gay population rights, and then watched as the "state tribe" took them back. The battle will always exist between, "The Will of the People", and "The Tags of the Tribe".

The Tag is all about staying the same. We can understand many things about our behaviour and others when we fully realize the impact of this statement. The Will calls us to experience life in many ways that would, and do, make our Tags panic. Our many Tags each desire to run the show from their interpretation of safety. With so many Tags created during our lives, they not only fight with The Will but with each other!

Let's follow the development of our first example with the child and build a mental picture of what is going on in the child's mind. Imagine that because of Parents Number Ones' messages, both obvious and tacit, the Self Referencing Guidance System, (The Protector) creates a Tag called "pest". Imagine if you would, a file created in the child's mind. An icon is created and on that icon, the Tag "pest" is inscribed. Inside the file is a script that says:

- "Asking questions will provoke a response from someone that may cause you harm."
- "People don't want to hear from you."
- "You are not important."
- "Be quiet and you will be safe."

This is the "code" that The Protector reads in order to produce the "appropriate" response in the child.

It is completely possible to have conflicting scripts, one saying we should, and the other saying we shouldn't do or say something. It is easy to feel conflicted with all the different positions occurring at once. The Tag with the greatest emotional impact, or the greatest perceived threat, will be the one that wins out in any given situation.

Stop for a moment and think about your reasons for buying this book. What was it that you were trying to learn about, change, or access? Why haven't you been able to do so in the past? Think about the times you wanted to lose weight, or take a chance at something new, go after that extra sale, ask for the raise, quit your job, hug a tree or whatever it was you desired, but then you did, thought, or felt otherwise. What about those feelings you get every time you walk into a room? "Is everyone looking at me? Are they approving or disapproving of me?"

If you examine the process, you will find that the behaviour that you exhibited and the feelings that you felt were strong enough to stop you from doing what it was you wanted to do. If you think back on it, you may even remember the inner dialogue where you skilfully talked yourself out of doing what it was you wanted to do.

All of the distractions that keep you from invoking your Will are the clever workings of Tags protecting themselves from being tampered with.

Recently, a client of mine, after spending about ninety minutes looking at her options in life, made a significant comment as she was leaving my office. Upon stepping out into the fresh air she said, "I feel naked." This had nothing to do with the temperature outside, nor was there a suggestion of embarrassment, or vulnerability. Her comment was an indication of the realization of the possibility of choice with which she was now empowered. She was expressing the feeling of an unencumbered lightness as she floated to her car.

During our encounter, she, (let's call her Sarah) expressed ideas similar to so many other you and I have heard over the years. She used words that reflected feelings of a self-worth, which were entirely qualified by opinions of others. Many of these opinions were garnered at an early age, as most of ours have been too. Like so many of us, these exterior opinions had become the lexicon from which she based "facts" about herself. Today, as a professional woman, Sarah was making life choices using these "facts" and, consequently, was feeling quite powerless.

She spoke of her own condemnation, for the anger she felt toward an individual who was actively abusive towards her. She felt that anger was an emotion for the weak or wicked and there was no room in her mind for justifiable anger. Any anger that she felt inside of her immediately triggered the Relationship Tag called "bad girl". To have anger, regardless of cause, was an indication to Sarah that she was a bad girl. She accepted this feeling without any conscious thought as to its validity or even its sanity.

As it turned out, that Relationship Tag was induced by a repressive father who saw any anger displayed by his children toward him as a flagrant attack on his authority. Of course, he had felt duty bound to quell any rebellion. This he carried out with a barrage of words and actions that left no doubt in the mind of the child of the negative consequences of anger, and conclusively, the dangerous nature of anger.

The process, with which Sarah went from an indentured slave of a Tag, to an effervescent spirit, occurred after I made her aware of the process whereby a Relationship Tag had become a fixed image of whom she was. She then went through a process, which we will discuss soon, which liberated her from the Tag, and used her Will to let go of the feelings that the Tag triggered in her.

Some other processes are involved to complete the scenario we are describing. To realize simply that our negative self-image is a Relationship Tag in disguise is certainly helpful because we no longer need say, "This is who I am." There is not one negative value of our self that we have to continue believing is an integral part of us. They are Tags as simple as that. They are mere labels affixed to our backs saying, "Kick me." Yes, our Protector treats them like a self-image and consequently protects them very strongly, and even reinforces them, but remember, The Will is our "God-given gift", and has the power to smite any Tag. We will get into the details of how to divest ourselves of this unwanted collateral. It will mean that we can stop claiming that they are a part of who we are, instead of something we happen to have. Then we will have the power to rid ourselves of them.

7

The Cowbird

One early spring on a particularly beautiful day, when the pungent smell of the earth and the songs of the birds gave notice that winter had finally surrendered her mantle, I witnessed a peculiar event. I was sitting on my back patio, drinking coffee and watching with odd amazement the antics of a bird that I did not recognize. This bird was all black except for its head, which was brown. I was later to find out that this two-toned creature was not an escapee from a science experiment, but an enterprising species known as the Cowbird. What made the behaviour so interesting was that Starlings already occupied the two birdhouses that I had built and erected amongst our trees. The female Cowbird, who is all brown, waited for the Starlings to go on an expedition and then entered their house.

Later on that week, I recounted my sighting to a friend of mine who works in a store that sells nature products (birdseed, binoculars, feeders, etc.). She told me that Cowbirds have an interesting solution to rearing their young. Cowbirds are "brood Parasites". Rather than going through the bother of nesting their young themselves, these surreptitious songsters deposit their eggs in another species' nests. Having done their deed, they leave, never to come back for babies' first flight or even graduation! When the egg hatches, the surrogate mother dutifully feeds the odd-looking offspring without the slightest notion that the "squawker" is someone else's night deposit.

There is a metaphor behind the story of the Cowbird, which fits right into the concept of Relationship Tags. Just like the new mother bird rearing its adopted young, there are ideas, concepts and beliefs that were, and still are, deposited into our heads without even the meekest objection from us. We care for and nurture these ideas until they become so much a part of our behaviour that we come to believe these ideas represent who we are. Why wouldn't we? We don't realize that they are being slipped right into our heads when we aren't looking.

"THROUGH THE DOOR!"

This is simply the way it is, because that's how our brain works. If I asked the meaning of the concept "6-down", you may be hard-pressed to find a definitive answer. Yet if I asked you the meaning of the concept "7-up", immediately the vision of a soft drink would come into your mind. Both phrases refer to a number and a direction, but one has been so permanently grafted to your mind by constant repetition and association to that green bottle or can, that it is virtually impossible for you to hear the phrase "7-up" without automatically thinking of it.

Of course, this is a benign example. We won't lose sleep over the idea of being induced to automatically conger up a soft drink in our minds. It is important, though, to realize that countless thousands of ideas have entered our minds by the same method. Many of these ideas are unconscious, and yet we act upon them every day. The ones we are the most interested in here are the ideas laid in our nests that then go on to form our supposed idea of self. Realize that, just like the adopting mother bird, we protect these ideas dutifully and efficiently, so much so that it is an automatic act that we do without question.

Think of some of your thoughts that you may have every day. What makes you think you couldn't learn about computers at your age? How do you know you can't fix the stove when the element is gone? Who said you couldn't be a good dancer? People allow so many of these "I can't's" to fall from their mouths that I can't help but call them "cowbird droppings."

Of course, to back up these ideas, we are systematically fed the proper feelings to ensure that we remain consistent to the Tag! These protections will automatically come up as Tag-feelings and behaviours, as we have said before, or with actions to preclude negative feelings from welling up. Why would we protect them? Because, as already covered earlier, the Self Referencing Guidance System has no way to differentiate between a true self-image and a Tag. Consequently, they all are nurtured, fed and protected. The difference between Tags and little Cowbirds is that the Tags never want to leave the nest!

Recently, a friend of old who had not heard me talking of these concepts before remarked with astonishment that I seemed to have become rather jaded, and had somehow lost the romance that emotions can bring. She saw my view of feelings as a reflection of someone perhaps trying to hide from feelings. I told her that nothing could be farther from the truth. In fact, the freedom to feel the joy that brings tears to the eye, for example, when seeing your daughter graduate, or simply being moved by a sunset, only happens when the Tags that say, "Men don't show emotions at things like that," is overruled. The Tags would rather produce embarrassment at being seen showing real emotions. There are actions such as tenderness, kindness, forgiveness, and compassion that come from the seat of the human soul that become stymied by Tags that teach us to be generally uncomfortable by these actions. That is why we generally are in awe of, people who can express those simple gestures.

Many thousands who never knew Mother Theresa revere her. Almost all they know of her is that she was a person who gave of herself without question to those who needed it. They are obviously not in love with a person they never knew; rather it's the idea of her, as a person doing her type of work that stirs them so much. We genuinely admire people like Mother Theresa because we recognize their real goodness and we validate it in our experience. It makes us feel good to know that there are people like that out there with the courage of their convictions. That says a lot about what is going on in our hearts, even if we don't act on it. We don't recognize things out there if they are not in us first. Most of us sense that what the Mother Theresa's in this world do is right; not right as opposed to wrong, but right in the sense that it is correct to follow one's heart and act on it. Not everyone is moved to do her work, but there are countless examples of how people rally together when needed to support people near and far when it really counts.

To my friend I say that my feelings are not jaded at all. Rather, I have a stronger sense of the real emotions and feelings that call to me to act from the heart, in spite of those defence emotions that would cower me. I do not trust emotions that tell me not to trust strangers all the time, that New Yorkers and Torontonians are all a cold bunch of people who will not give you the time of day. Emotions that would chide me for laughing too loud, or crying at a tender moment in a movie all have an agenda that has to do with tribal noise.

Imagine if we could make an itemized list of all the things we do in a day, and then add up the time spent on Tags, (assuming of course that we reach the stage where we would admit that certain things were Tag-behaviour). We would be quite shocked to discover that as much as 95% of our daily activities are spent in Tag maintenance. Remember, it is not just the activity we are doing directly which stems from Tag-behaviour, but if we are doing it to avoid doing others things for which Tags say no – then it is a Tag-behaviour.

With this in mind, how many people are in the job they want? How many people are in the relationships they want? Are you in a perfectly good job that you hate? Are you being a good provider, while denying yourself the chance to be where you want to be? If so, then that is also Tag-behaviour. You are protecting your cowbird droppings as if they were manna from heaven!

Did you know that the people who run correspondence schools would go out of business if more than just a few percent of the people actually finished their courses? The schools know that almost no-one finishes the courses that they start. People have all the right motives when they sign up for these courses. But the never-ceasing voices in their heads, telling them all the reasons why it was a bad idea to have gotten the course, finally convince them that they can at least come out of the situation okay if they just don't finish it.

Often we do try to break away from the Tags. Taking courses to enrich ourselves, trying to start our own business on the side, taking dancing lessons, all of these are attempts to break away from the Tags that would hold us in place. The number of people who wish they could just quit their job is quite high. Many people succeed in the attempt, it is true, but the greater majority of us never start, and even more never finish.

It would be at this point when your Tags may kick in heavily and whisper in your ear thoughts encouraging you to dismiss this whole concept outright.

The Tag-feelings will always whisper these things to us, like the devil in the cartoons that jumps up on our shoulder and whispers in our left ear. Most of the time, between the "Go for it", and the "Think of everyone else" that is bounced back and forth in our heads, we do

THE COWBIRD

little. Consequently, the little "angel" sends us a "That's a good boy or girl" message. "Yes, we can feel cheated in life, but at least look at how the world will applaud our steadfastness!"

The hardest part in telling you these ideas, is that it is impossible to get you alone so that I can talk to just you. Your Tags are always listening, which means that there are hundreds of other versions of you in your head, reading this at the same time as you are, and going on alert.

Cowbirds are not "bad" parents. They are not abandoning their children. They do not posses the capacities to make these or any other judgments. They are merely following instincts. Their act of leaving their eggs in another bird's nest is unusual, but it gets the job of survival done.

So too, the majority of the Tags in our heads did not get there by malicious intent, but were grafted on as a part of our survival system. They are not sentient things possessing independent thinking that allows them to realize that the world of their origin is long gone. Their source of information, and the process by which they get their information, have changed dramatically, and yet the system operates as if the individual has no capacity to distinguish between opinion and reality.

Indeed, as a child, the opinion of others means everything. By the time we grow into our sense of self-awareness, the, who that is us, is coated over with so many layers of injunctions covering all activities that we can barely move on our own behalf. They got there by absorbing other people's belief systems and coping mechanisms; but belief systems is all that they are. Some of them work well, and others do not work at all. They were given to us directly and indirectly, but being given something does not mean that we have to keep it. More importantly, being given something doesn't make it something we become; it is merely something that we have.

As mentioned earlier in the book, that which we think of as ours, we protect. Of those things that we disown, we feel no attachment for them. That is why we say, "I'm taking out the garbage," and not, "…taking out my garbage."

"THROUGH THE DOOR!"

In order to get rid of the cowbird droppings in our nest, we must first start by removing the birds. Once we do that, we can take care of the stuff left behind. It is infinitely simpler to face the Tags rather than fighting their shadows, the emotions. Our task then is to effectively eliminate the Tags, and let the emotions and feelings that they trigger lose their potency.

8

Sticks and Stones…

I remember in the early seventies taking physics at the University of Toronto. My professor whisked through the concepts of Newtonian mechanics, wave theory, and the nature of light and so on. When we came to the end of the term, the subject turned to Quantum Mechanics. One of the things I noticed the most about my professor was the change in his manner of teaching. There was a definite loss of poise, and his voice lacked the certainty that comes from being "at one" with one's work.

Discussions of the Heisenberg Uncertainty Principle, and the nature of matter, started to sound less like a course based on absolute principles, and more like a dissertation of Far Eastern spiritualism. It seemed that according to this "exact" science, human thought could play a direct role in the location, or even the existence, of the building blocks of all matter. It seemed that the decision to look for a certain particle in an experiment caused a direct change in the outcome. Our thoughts affected matter and energy itself at the atomic level. These were not mystical ideas or philosophy, but hardened science.

I remember my reaction to this information. For several years, I had been questioning religion and my beliefs and finding me pulling away from dogma that I had been asked to accept without thought. Now, years later, the scientists whom I had replaced as priests in the myth of life were themselves questioning their religion of science. I turned to those books that tried to make us see the nature of matter in a way that lay people could understand. Books like The Tao of Physics, by Fritjof Capra, and The Dancing Wu Li Masters by Gary Zukav were the beginning. In my search for the "truth", I needed to discover where the "good guys" were. These scientists had been, up to then, my David, slayer of the giant that was my former religion. Now it seemed that David was himself slain by a new master come to free the wandering tribes. These books tore asunder my naive solace in the laws of science; for now science had lost its precise, calculable, and predictable edge. The problem was that I could not simply dismiss the facts because I didn't like them. That would be the least scientific act of all.

The consequence of looking at the parallels of quantum mechanics and eastern spiritualism was to make me conscious of my own thinking. Specifically how that thinking influenced our lives. It's been many years since that physics class. In my mind, there is no question but that we play a supporting role in creating our reality, and the reality that we see around us. Research every day gives us tangible evidence of the effect we have on creating the world around us as individuals and as tribes, and the direct consequence of our thinking on the human body. We use biofeedback to control our heart rate, alter our brain waves, and produce relaxation states in the body by changing the hormone secretions from the brain. Studies have shown that even in physical training, the way we think can strongly affect the outcome.

The consequences of the fact that our mind makes no distinction between what is out there in the physical world and what is in our thoughts should be made very clear to everyone. This is one of those simple, yet very powerful life-changing truths.

If (as facts show), when we specifically set out to control the body through the mind by thought alone, and as a consequence our physical body responds as if the stimulus was external, then we must conclude that our thinking affects our body and our feelings and the way we see ourselves. Even when we are not conscious of what our thoughts are creating, the creation goes on nevertheless! So, without consciousness, what does control our thoughts? Tags!

It then becomes not:

"You are what you eat."

Rather it is more:

"You are what you think eating is going to make you!"

In other words, our thoughts are always having a direct physical (i.e. matter) effect on ourselves. We can say, therefore, that our thoughts do indeed matter. The direct relationship between energy and matter as discussed in physics applies here to thought. Thoughts spawn activity in a brain that manufactures enzymes and triggers chemicals as needed to make the body follow its dictates. They create matter by making our thoughts a physical reality.

When something happens to someone that causes them to feel disappointment, say losing a promotion or missing an opportunity, one might, in an attempt to cover feelings respond, "Oh, it doesn't matter." In real absolute terms, those feelings matter a great deal. Our physical and emotional selves respond to, and are chemically altered by our thoughts. By using instruments that measure blood pressure, and hormone secretions in the body, these instruments tell us quite readily that our bodies are physically not the same anymore due to the thought, which transformed the energy we put into matter, where none was there before.

This concept, when viewed beside Relationship Tags, takes on a new meaning. Because thoughts are things, and create physiological changes in our bodies, our bodies respond directly not only to the thoughts we are thinking, but also to the ongoing, subconscious attitudes and beliefs that we hold as true. Since many of our beliefs spring from Relationship tags, we can start to see that even our physical bodies have responded to the tags, and are perpetually recreating themselves to the underlying visions we hold of ourselves. We are then constantly reinforcing these ideas by our thoughts and actions.

We see the result of this every day in our ability to discern the meek from the self-assured. The victim personality sticks out in a crowd walking around suspiciously with eyes darting and hands clutched tightly. Any good actor, when asked to portray a personality type, will assume certain postures and antics that are indicative of the personality that we all recognize. Why are they so identifiable? It is because our body assumes standard positions of the attitude that dominates.

That is why body language is the strongest and most authentic reflection of what a person believes behind the words spoken. Watch commercials where an actor is promoting a certain product and see if her head is shaking "No" when she is telling you how much she likes the product. The body doesn't lie!

"THROUGH THE DOOR!"

By accepting Relationship Tags as a part of who we are, our physiology and psychology align themselves to these ideas and matter is transformed into the image that reflects them. Our "selves" become the "matter of fact" reflections of these ideas, but the facts themselves are merely beliefs in ideas that mostly came from outside of us – the Relationship Tag.

We must understand that ideas literally shape us in ways that we may or may not find acceptable to our Will. In the absence of our Will's decision to change them, they become the shape of things to come. It is not "Seeing is believing." It is "Believing is seeing!" What we believe, we have become. We have not made our selves conscious of the fact that we can choose what we believe. Since were told to believe 95% plus of what we believe about ourselves we, it is a great effort to recreate our selves into the image that we want to be.

What is the alternative? The alternative is a life of unconscious adherence to actions and attitudes, which may or may not have our dreams and desires as part of the package. The choice is simple, but it requires our presence.

Everything in life matters. All that comes to our senses is transformed from basic sensory input to information by our minds, which then respond physically to it. The childhood retort, "Sticks and stones may break my bones but names will never hurt me," is a brave comeback for a child but it is hardly a statement of fact. The sticks and stone wounds of our youth have long ago been healed and forgotten, but those names are the cornerstone of many frozen dreams and unhappiness. Of course, names themselves are just words, and we do have the choice to accept or reject the names, but little children who are all dependent upon those giants called parents have a strong biological injunction to adhere to the dictates of their life-giving progenitors.

In other words, ridicule a child enough and that ridicule becomes a fact, and the Tag is created. We are not here to condemn the labellers, because this isn't about them. Our interest is in the choices we can make now. What we need is to become aware that this is a process. It occurs and continues to occur without the presence of a conscious Will to change it.

STICKS AND STONES...

What is the matter with us is what we make matter. All those solidified (made into matter) thoughts created in the past are recreated moment by moment by self-images. They continue to think into existence their version of us, without our conscious awareness that it is going on. Without a constant creative process occurring in our system of mind, body, and spirit, our bodies would start to decay. All those molecules of hydrogen, carbon, oxygen etc., which make up our bodies, are there because the essence of us has summoned them to make us into matter. The building blocks of matter are constantly attracted together by the force of intent, and so they stay. When we die, the molecules themselves don't disintegrate, but with no one there, willing them to stay together, they naturally dismember and slowly go off on their own. Thus, we say that the body decays, but not the substance that forms it.

We generally believe that our bodies are created at the time of conception, and then a pinch of environment is added to the mix to produce the result that we call us. The reality is very different. At every moment, we create our bodies from the specifications of our present collective thoughts and beliefs coming from all parts of our being!

The free will given to us by the gods is truly free, and it allows us to create whatever image we have of ourselves. All of our thoughts consequently are consulted. Our conscious thoughts, our unconscious thoughts, our desires, fears, dreams, beliefs, and our self-images/Tags, all go into the mix that creates the physical us. Because our relationship tags form the greatest bulk of our unconscious thought, the essence of our being is constantly re-created repeatedly every instant by the same recipe called on by the Relationship Tags. This gives us the illusion of the self that eventually grows old and dies.

It would be a capricious god that would give us free will, and then sabotage it with a built-in system that overrides it. Fortunately for us, this is not so. Free will is lazy, but it does have the ability and the means to tell the Tags to go to hell. Since the Tags have a strong habit of taking us to hell with them, and making us feel all sorts of Tag-feelings when we don't listen to them, we relent and let the Tags win. This is our free choice and we hate to admit that we are a party to our Tags' whims, so we invent all sorts of blame which we bestow on our parents, kids, bosses, weather, money, government, the red, black, white, tall, etc…

It would be a fascinating experience for you to record your conversations for a whole day and then play them back with an open-eyed consciousness. Sorting out the sentences into the various categories would probably be a shocking experience for you. The categories that would show up more often would be:

- Things I say which undermine me.
- Things I say that reinforce the "tribe" but take away from my sense of self.
- Things I say that I know are not true but give me a false sense of importance.
- Things I say that put me down so that others won't think that I think I'm important.
- Things I say to put others down so that I will feel important – in my own mind at least!
- Things I say just to be liked.

At the end of the exercise, you would discover that what passes as conversation and communication often has more to do with positioning and reinforcement of your idea of self than a true expression of which you really are. The intent of the topics of conversation, the reason people speak up in the first place, has a lot to do with the positioning of a person within the particular tribe he or she happens to be in that day.

Even as a motivational management consultant working with very successful corporations, I saw business meetings that were nothing more than tribal adjustments. An interlocking of horns, if you will, to establish power and position.

We may think that much of our day is spent looking after ourselves. In fact, much of our time is spent looking after our "selves" – those many different Tag versions of us that wish to keep us safe from all possible harm, and like an overprotective parent, dress us up for every possible scenario until, burdened by the weight of protection, we cannot move.

What we call reality today, those things that we can touch, feel and experience, is mostly the result of a very gifted and clever mind with the capacity to turn anything into the reality of our choosing. Most of the time, everyone (the tribe) chooses the same thing and so most people tend to see a similar world. The few individuals who broke from the tribe, Jesus, Siddhartha, Gandhi, Einstein, Michelangelo, Copernicus, Newton and friends, created realities so compelling that we made them ours, and the world changed as a consequence.

What really matters to you? What is it that springs from within? What is it that, in spite of all feelings that attempt to hold you back, still sneaks out from time to time and begs your attention? Thought creates matter. What matters to you seeks expression even as the Tag-feelings tease and cajole you into inaction. There is a way around this ageless defence. The solution to the tug-of-war is not to pull harder, but to let go of the rope and walk away from the game.

What we have done so far is to open the closet door and expose to the light the process that runs our unconscious lives. Now we will reveal another system, the most clever of them all, which until now has been the fodder of poets and psychologists. This scoundrel and snake oil peddler has engaged us all our lives in the shell game I like to call Shadowboxing.

9

"Me and My…Shadow…"

Did you ever wonder how a 150-pound human could control a 4000-pound elephant? In 1982, I was traveling through India. One of my stops was in Hyderabad, where I was a guest of the police commissioner there. Among the tremendous tour of the city that he arranged for me was a trip to the Hyderabad Zoo, which is the largest zoo in Asia. I remember being rather amazed as I walked past an elephant not more than 20 feet away from me. This huge animal was chained to a very small stake in the ground. I knew that any elephant a quarter of its size could easily pull that stake right out of the ground. So I asked my host why the elephant surrendered its Will so easily to the stake. The commissioner told me that the elephant is put on a stake at a very early age, when physically it is not able to remove the stake out of the ground. It tries to pull at it but cannot succeed. Consequently, the young elephant learns that the stake is stronger than it is. When the elephant becomes older and stronger, it never again tries to pull the stake out of the ground because of what it has learned. What it learned as a child imprints on its self-image and so the elephant becomes a prisoner, not of the stake, but of its relationship to the stake.

That is a perfect description of a Relationship Tag at work. It is in the design of the minds of many animals to learn this way. It is not in the capacity of the elephant to question what it believes, and so the Tag is protected and consequently controls the elephant's way of thinking

Humans learn things and develop Tags the same way as our elephant friend does. Additionally, because of our language, we have the ability to question what we are doing. If it was any one of us tied to the stake from birth, we might not actually figure out ourselves that we had become big enough to pull the stake out, but if someone came up to us and explained the logic, chances are we would then try. Often in life that is exactly what happens. Whenever we read an inspiring book, or we see others doing something we never thought we could do, it

67

gives us enough encouragement to start in that direction. All the important changes we have made in our lives we made because of our decision to pull at the stake even if we believed it was too strong for us. We chanced it and then – it snapped and we were free.

Many times, even in these situations, if we haven't generated enough momentum to succeed, one of two things happen. We either stall the initiation of the process until we forgot about it, or we start with great gusto, but with an obstacle here, or a little problem there, we eventually wind down our initial eagerness and stop doing what was working. Then we find all sorts of "reasons" why it wouldn't have worked in the first place.

Why is this behaviour so common and so predictable? The Tags, we must not forget, are a part of The Protector and are very entrenched, and their need to protect themselves is very strong. From what we have learned of Relationship Tags, if it could be so easy to motivate someone to move in a direction away from them, it would greatly compromise their ability to protect us in the early stages of our development.

In order to be able to maintain a truly functional input into the survival of man after the onset of self-awareness, The Protector had to develop a way to try to keep us from tampering with its line of defence. All it had to do was to take something it already had and adapt it to challenge the new would-be-king, The Will. From its bag of tricks, The Protector came up with the wiliest of all weapons – tag-feelings!

We observe an array of emotions in animals. They can muster anger when provoked, they can exhibit fear when threatened, a mother can look frantic and worried when her young has gone missing. You can even see their happiness in certain situations. Nevertheless, there are certain feelings that require self-awareness to function, and are therefore absent in animals other than man. These feelings are shame, guilt, embarrassment, stupidity, awkwardness, ugliness, and a host of descriptive adjectives that trigger uncomfortable feelings within us.

What these feelings have in common other than being strictly human is that they are all conceptual and judgmental. Truly, they are Tag-feelings. In other words, these feelings are post self-awareness feelings that have come about because of man's ability to reflect on his own thoughts and then make judgments. These feelings all have the property of letting us suspend rationale, causing us to act in various ways that defy The Will.

Let's look at the situation described in Chapter 6 regarding Sarah and her father. We have been around as a species for a long time and we have learned a thing or two about survival since then. Imagine Sarah, as a young child whose father so strongly abused her. Because his self-esteem was so injured, he couldn't stand to see his child express any anger towards him. This was a direct threat to his "masculinity" and he dealt with it. It doesn't take much insight to realize that if Sarah continued to express her anger to such a man, that it could develop into a potentially dangerous situation for her. Her mind therefore took this information and stored it as survival information. Her father essentially tagged her with a label of "trouble maker" and pest. This, then, became strongly entrenched in her, not because it was true, but because her father strongly indicated that it was in her best interest to think that way. The Protector concurred!

The part played by the father was to give Sarah the appropriate (to him) label or Tag. Please note that this label in the past is what we would have called a self-image. It now became the task of Sarah's mind to do something with the Tag. What it did was store the information as survival data. Just like the experience of touching something red hot would make us automatically wary of anything red that is giving off heat, (e.g. another stove element), this label has a warning written on it that says if Sarah expresses her anger, she could be in serious trouble. Her mind therefore simply took the anger (the cause of being threatened), and put it out of her mind and into her body to protect her from using it to her peril. The fact is, we are realizing more and more the nature of illnesses and how directly related it is to the way we think. This is a good clue as to what will happen. Sarah now becomes an outwardly passive individual who becomes easy to take advantage of because she doesn't rock the boat. To this particular Tag, though, the little girl is safe.

Whenever you hear about battered women staying with their abusers in spite of what they know to be better, think of Sarah and see that the Tag is doing what it can to protect itself, and indirectly, is protecting the individual. Tags are a blind response system that does not judge. As we have said earlier, the Self Referencing Guidance System is a non-judgmental data collector that can only draw non-judgmental conclusions. The Protector has no way of knowing the difference between Tags when they arrived on the scene, and self-images. Please see that if you had a Tag called "worthless", the job of the Tag would be to keep you thinking that way. It would erroneously conclude that it was in your best survival interest to preserve that thought and attempt to stop you any other time you attempted to think any other way. The reason for this is that the Tag sees you forever as who you were at the time of its creation. A Tag created when you were six years old will forever see you as a six year old, and try to protect the six year old in you. It is your Will that desires to be different, and your Tags that work to keep you where you are.

Think about Tag-feelings. Take embarrassment, shame, anger, and ridicule. These are feelings that people try to avoid; sometimes at great cost. There are many things we will not do out of fear of triggering these feelings, and I'm not talking about those death-defying acts like bungee jumping. When surveyed and asked to rate various situations in terms of the amount of fear they instil, most people will place the act of public speaking as the number one situation. Death only comes in later on the list. The fears caused by the idea of public speaking are completely removed from any true consequence in nature and it is easy to see how they are created in response to an idea rather than anything in the "real world"

Why do we avoid these feelings so strongly that we will go to so much pain to avoid them? More importantly, what is the consequence of this avoidance?

Do you remember Maslow's pyramid? He said that survival is the first priority of the mind, and that it screens all information for this possibility. Therefore, whenever an event comes up that triggers a Tag, the mind sounds the alarm and instantly alerts the army which either rewards us for listening to the Tag, or gives us a warning that we are about to cross the defences of the Tag and leave our self unprotected. These soldiers of the mind are the Tag-feelings

"ME, AND MY...SHADOW"

It may seem cold, or at the very least mechanistic, to think of feelings as a reward/punishment device of the subconscious, but it is a model of understanding which can put into perspective our actions, especially the ones where we find our self acting counter to our own desires.

Here is a way to visualize the process. Imagine the opening of a movie where you see a woman in front of a store window, staring at a dress. The scene changes to inside her head where you see a Relationship Tag, relaxing on a lounge chair at the beach with a drink in its hand. Its job is simply to make sure that the woman doesn't cross the line that could threaten its existence. Since people change very little Tags have a lot of free time. The scene changes back to the woman, who by now is inside the store examining the dress and thinking that she might actually look quite good in it. Inside her head an alarm sounds, and the Relationship Tag puts down his drink and calmly selects a button on the lounge chair called guilt. The woman suddenly starts talking to herself.

"Oh, I shouldn't really; it's much too expensive and besides, Billy could use some new running shoes for school."

The woman sighs and quietly puts the dress back on the rack and walks out the store. As she leaves, we hear her muttering to herself, "It's probably for the best." The Relationship Tag satisfied that the guilt tactic was sufficient, picks up its drink, sits back and enjoys the sun

All the Tag has to do for the most part is trigger in us an uncomfortable emotion and we step back in line. The Tag may even, in the case of the woman just mentioned, give her a good-feeling reward for sublimating her own desires and thinking about others first. In this way, the Tag has very little to do, because the feelings it evokes will do most of the work. The Tag, which in this case could be titled, "Don't think of yourself", or "You come last – way, way last" or even, "What makes you think you deserve anything?" is never addressed. The woman is only aware of the desire for the dress, the feeling of guilt it produced, and the tidbit she received for not buying the dress in the end. The Relationship Tag, protected by the emotion of guilt in this case, is never seen.

Why did she not buy the dress? Not because of Billy's shoes, and not because she didn't need the dress. The important thing to understand is that she didn't buy the dress because of any thought process where she consciously said to herself that she doesn't deserve it. It was the threat of feeling the subsequent feelings the Tag would have released on her if she bought the dress! If we were to sum this up, we would say:

The Tags do not stop you themselves. Your feelings the Tags trigger stop you. You are manipulated into following Tags because of the of the Tag's effects; the cause doesn't even have to be visible.

Every Tag in our heads is very well protected. They are so well hidden in our minds that often we only ever see the shadow they cast. These shadows are the Tag-feelings. Our Tags are very rarely identified or transgressed, but the emotional shadows are around us all the time. Most of our attempts to change and improve ourselves actually involve trying to get rid of the way the Tags make us feel. Getting rid of fear, anger, shame, etc. is not getting rid of the Tags! These are the Tag's shadows. This is the catch-22 in most personal growth or self-development courses and books. People think that they are actually changing their self-image when in fact they are shadowboxing!

All the activities we do to "get in touch with our feelings" are activities focused on the effects of the Tags, not the Tags themselves. When I see clients who tell me that they are so afraid of this or guilty of that, their ardent desire is to rid themselves of the emotional response that the Tag triggers. We have a strong aversion to feeling shame, guilt or embarrassment etc., and therefore do all sorts of things to avoid these feelings. Importantly, it is the Tag that creates these feelings in order to keep us following a certain, predictable, "safe" pattern of behaviour.

When we hear of people who are "getting in touch with their feelings", what they are actually doing is focusing on the shadows of their problem, but not the problem itself. No one in his or her right mind, when being attacked by a dog, would try to defend him or herself by jumping on the dog's shadow; but that is exactly what the "therapies" that focus on "tuning into feelings" are doing.

The Tag-feelings are there to protect the Tag by doing any or all of the following:

- Instilling a feeling in us that we find uncomfortable which makes us back off from any attempt to break through a Tag.
- Making us avoid situations altogether such that the emotion won't even come up.
- Giving us a token reward (a good feeling) for not breaking through a Tag.
- In the end, changing the subject so that the subject now is the emotion we want to avoid, rather than the Tag we want to break through.

When I hear people say that they are doing such and such therapy to get in touch with their feelings, in my mind the word "gotcha" pops up. This is when I know that a Tag is so successfully entrenched in a person's belief system. They will now spend days, months, and years, focussed on the emotion that the Tag found useful in keeping them from transgressing. Thus, the battle is with the shadow, while King Tag sits comfortably and safely in its place, getting the pawns to do the work.

What happens after all the time, effort and money has been spent to get in touch with the feelings of, say, being undeserving? The Tag merely uses a different emotion to work on, or goes to level two of protection. It makes us ill, so that we still cannot transgress the Tag!

The term Shadowboxing, as many people know, is a boxing term that refers to the practice of boxers boxing with their shadows on a wall. Every time they hit the wall, they are hitting the glove of their shadow counterpart. Of course, the harder and faster they hit the shadow, the harder and faster it hits back. You can never defeat your shadow because you are the animator of it. Likewise, the harder you try to fight your feelings, the more energy you give them. Try This. Don't think of a pink elephant in spandex. My guess is there is some image in your mind of a prancing pink pachyderm. You can't eliminate something in the mind by focusing on it, or even trying not to think of it. It only becomes more powerful. Look at this example:

Dan is at a dance, talking with his friend Mark. He sees Liz over in the corner just standing around with some other girls. He really wants to dance with her, and by chance, she secretly really wants to dance with him. His friend whispers to him to go and ask her to dance.

He, of course, says, "No, I can't. She probably doesn't like me."

"Well go and find out," chides his friend.

"No I just can't. I'm too shy!" says Dan.

"Do it anyway," returns the friend.

"I'll be too embarrassed," admits Dan.

In our boy-doesn't-meet-girl scenario, the message from Dan is clear.

"I can't do this because the emotion of possible rejection has overpowered my desire to dance with Liz."

Of course the Tag, and it could be any number of them, never comes up. It could be Dan's belief that he is not good enough, that girls don't like him, or that he is too tall/small/fat/skinny/poor/uncoordinated/goofy/uncool etc. Any of these ideas are challengeable in a court of common sense. So what is it that actually stops Dan? Not the Tag, but the shadow cast by it – the possible feeling of rejection.

Think about those things that you would like to do, or say, or be, etc., and think about what is really stopping you. Underneath any of the fluff excuses is the fear of feeling a Tag-feeling! We are so fearful of these feelings that we mould, shape and bend our behaviour to avoid even thinking about them.

Why do most people rate public speaking as more frightening than death? If we can really understand this one, then we will have taken one major step through the door. People are not afraid of public speaking because they will make a fool of themselves, or they will look stupid, or people will laugh at them. They are afraid of public speaking because of the way the Tags makes them feel about even thinking about doing it. The Tags do this in order to prevent people from public speaking when it violates a Tag about who they are.

In other words, they are not afraid of being laughed at; they're afraid of how they are going to feel if they are laughed at.

Do you see the difference? It's the feelings that they are trying to avoid! They don't even have to get into details of why they feel people would laugh at them.

The reason why public speaking evokes such strong fears is that we were all given many Tags that have to do with the importance we should place on what other people think about us. In public speaking, we have the opportunity to "screw up" so many of these Tags. Just think of women going out with rollers in their hair, or men going out with a suit on and running shoes. How about standing up in a subway or bus and telling a joke to everyone? Many harmless acts can trigger embarrassment in people; precisely because of the feelings that even the idea of doing these things would evoke is very strong.

Therefore, we shadowbox! The focus of so much of our attention in life, consciously or unconsciously, is on these Tag-feelings. People, as we've said before, go to all sorts of counselling to get in touch with their feelings. Meanwhile the culprit which sends out the feeling, the Tag, is safely tucked away in their heads, running their lives and getting away with it most of the time.

Even those strong individuals who really desire to change their lives and decide to fight their feelings are involved in shadowboxing. Remember when the boxer hits the wall harder, he is hit back just as hard. So too it is when people spend their energy and time getting in touch with their feelings, trying to get their feelings to go away, or facing the feelings; they are still focused on the feelings.

The feelings are not the problem; they are the consequence of the problem. As long as people spend their energy on their Tag-feelings, they will only serve to reinforce the Tags even more. The only solution to a problem is the solution. That seems like an obvious and maybe superfluous thing to say, but if you walk into a room and you see someone hitting their head against the wall while complaining of a headache, their solution is not an aspirin. Yes, an aspirin or two can take away a headache, but you wouldn't start by eliminating the pain, you would start by suggesting that the individual stop hitting his head! The only way to get rid of the Tag, then, is by getting rid of the Tag!

"THROUGH THE DOOR!"

The problem for everyone is that it is the feelings the Tags trigger in us which are visible and uncomfortable. In other words, the cause is invisible but the effects are glaring. We want to stop the pain in our head, but don't make the connection with the banging of our head on the wall with the pain. Also, as we have seen in the idea of shadowboxing that the more you focus on an emotion, the more you feed it. We must get it through our heads (in order to get it out) that the Tag is the thing we must tackle!

The next time we hear someone say, "I'm so stupid, I couldn't do it," see that it is not the being stupid that is the problem; it's the feeling of being stupid that is the problem. No one wants to feel stupid, because it hurts. You may not change from feeling stupid right away, but you can examine the reasons why you think you are stupid in the first place and do something with that. Being called stupid when you were little does not make it so, except in your mind. Fighting the feeling saps all your energy.

Going through the door happens when you can say, "I don't care what I feel. I know that I can't possibly be as stupid as I feel; therefore, in spite of my feelings, I will pursue my desires because that is what I Will do, in spite of any feelings to the contrary." Waiting for the feelings to go away before you act could take you a lifetime and that's just what the Tags have in mind!

Now we have separated the self from the Tag, and we know the difference. We see that Tags cause us to act in a certain way by threatening us with the Tag-feelings that we really want to avoid. It explains why we feel guilt, shame, embarrassment and many other feelings about ourselves.

What we will now to describe is how this comes together to produce the strangest aspect of our behaviour. This behaviour sends most people to psychologists for help, and is directly related to Tags. It is fortunately now the simplest thing to identify, and choose to overcome. Ladies and gentlemen: The self-image Paradox…

10

The Self-Image Paradox

We are creatures of habit. Let's face it – habits are convenient. Not having to readdress the issue of the food we like or don't like each time we eat, or having to remind ourselves every day to drive on the correct side of the road, speeds up our lives and makes them nicely predictable and safe. The manner in which we greet people when we first meet them is usually habitual, and so are many of the things we do each day.

Another term for habit is unconscious behaviour. If we are not thinking about it, then it is an unconscious deed. We spend much of our time in an unconscious mode. So much so that when we speak, we rarely listen to what we, ourselves, are saying. In casual conversation, we blurt out sayings, mottoes, and clichés without any thought of their real relevance. Clichés, in fact, have the task of providing automatic responses to statements so that we don't have to think of something to say.

This unconscious, or habitual, mode is nothing other than Relationship Tags running the show. The indication that we are living mostly via our self-images, rather than our Will, can be inferred by how habitual our lives are.

As we have said, self-images never shut off, and never turn their attention elsewhere. They are always vigilant in their attempts to keep us exactly as we are.

The existence of a process that actively works against the wishes of consciousness produces the most extraordinary paradox. This paradox affects us every day, and is so ingrained in our daily lives, yet there is no term for it in everyday conversation. I have dubbed this curiosity "The self-image Paradox".

The self-image Paradox (S.I.P.) describes the process and explains the seemingly contrary behaviours we possess. When we understand the way the paradox works, our behaviours become quite understandable.

"THROUGH THE DOOR!"

The self-image Paradox:

1. All of our gains mean a change in our lives.
2. The mind automatically compares the change with the values of our self-images.
3. If the change is counter to the values of the self-image, that self-image will see the gain as a threat.
4. Our self-image will immediately attempt to thwart the gain, in spite of our real desire to have it.

The power that comes with the understanding of these four sentences is tremendous. Within its framework is the map that shows the way into the dilemma and the road out. Let us now venture down the road and explore the territory.

All of our gains mean a change in our life.

This may seem obvious, and if so, we can venture from the known into the more complex. The way a gain can change our life depends upon the nature and intensity of the gain. Winning a million dollars is certainly a huge gain to most people and unquestionably changes a person's life. The priorities shift, concerns change, social status is altered, etc.

Getting a degree, a new job, a promotion and falling in love, are all gains with the potential of lifelong changes. In a less obvious way, a smile from a stranger, someone opening the door for us, and the stranger giving up a seat on the bus for us – these are also gains. In that moment that they occur, they all give us something. It is recognition, and an acknowledgement of our existence. It is gratifying and feeds into our need for social interaction and acceptance.

Therefore, a gain can be trivial, instantaneous, immense, and/or life changing. Regardless of the quality or quantity of the gain, these changes automatically undergo part two.

The mind automatically compares the change with the values of our self-images.

THE SELF IMAGE PARADOX

This is an automatic and autonomic process. In other words, it happens without our conscious consent. Every one of our self-images, as we have stated before, has a precise framework. By using the term self-images here, we are including the three aspects that make up what we term self-image:

- The Will
- The Protector
- The Relationship Tag

The self-image that deals with our general self-worth knows exactly what is beneath it or above it.

Because it is a conclusion, it has concluded or finalized the picture. That automatically makes it easy for it to appraise quickly any event as either within or without its boundaries. This leads us to:

If the change is counter to the values of the self-image, that self-image will see the gain as a threat.

In other words, because of the comparing, the self-image will identify and tag anything outside of its limits as something it must act upon and eliminate.

Our self-image will immediately attempt to thwart the gain, in spite of our real desire to have that gain.

This is the moment where we enter into the realm of havoc. All of sudden we find our self in a situation where guilt, shame, embarrassment, fear, or any other disabling feeling invades conscious thought and causes us to reflect upon our gain in a different light.

For example:

From out of the blue, you are offered a promotion or a new job that will mean a substantial increase in your salary and your responsibilities. This is something you find exciting and full of possibilities. Your mind, after quickly running through 1-3 of the S.I.P. concludes that the money you will make is above the level of your self-worth image. At the same time, your self-image that deals with your ability to handle this kind of responsibility, regards you as overstepping the self-image boundary. Now the S.I.P. goes to work.

You may start out really wanting the job or promotion; however, you start having second thoughts. If you take the job, friends may get jealous. You may start to think about the extra taxes you will have to pay, and the responsibility that that entails. You may get a flashback to when you were young and spent all your money on candy and then got sick.

It is also possible that absolutely no thinking process occurs. You may simply start feeling an unaccountable feeling of dread and impending doom. Emotions arise that are so strong; you make a connection with the feeling and the job offer.

You then rationalize the reason why you are happy with your present job, and after all, who needs all that extra work? You start feeling calmer, relaxed and in control, which then reinforces your decision not to take that job. The self-image has done its job and stands down from Red Alert.

These events go on every day. Most of the time, our self-images are at work on areas of our lives that are little noticed. Things such as thinking that someone wants something from us because they opened the door for us, or downplaying a compliment by saying, "It was nothing" are examples of our Relationship Tags at work.

These situations follow the same process as previously described. They can happen so fast that we pay them no mind. They can happen 10-20-30 or 40 times per day. The paradox is that they all happened in spite of what we want.

You may really believe you deserve a promotion, but feel too frightened to discuss it. You may really want to ask him to dance, but you feel too shy to ask. You may want to tell someone off, but you feel too insecure to do so.

The S.I.P. demonstrates to us that our self-images can be quite contrary to our desires. It indicates then, that if they can go against what we want, they must not be what we would consider us. The good news from this is the realization that —we are not our self-images.

You are the person who is reading this now, even though your self-images may go on red alert because of it. If you are the person who controls, decides, and evokes your Will, you are the person who can say:

THE SELF IMAGE PARADOX

"In spite of feeling that I can't handle the promotion, I really know deep down inside that I can. I want it, so I'll take it and deal with my feelings as I go along."

Know then, that the S.I.P. means that a lot of what happens in your life is dictated by that automatic process that controls what you do, how you think, and what emotions you should be using at any given time. It also means that much of what you do in your life has nothing to do with YOU!

You may choose to see this as bad new that your life has been spent doing much of what isn't reflected in whom you are. Alternately, you could see this as great news! It implies that the life ahead of you can be filled with different decisions, different experiences, and the opportunity to express your true self as you walk through the door.

Fortunately, for all of us, there is a way around the self-image-Paradox. We can't shut it off, but because we are human, we have that one capacity that is stronger than the S.I.P., and that is the Human Will.

The Children of The Will

The desires to grow intellectually, emotionally, and spiritually, are the children of The Will. There is a big difference in wanting to achieve a goal based on The Will's desire to succeed, and the frenetic urgency of someone whose Tag is threatening him or her with the label of "failure" if they don't "do it better than everyone else."

Success in our lives, the feeling that we are living life by our wishes and desires then, is a reflection of our capacity to overcome the self-images that would keep us from change.

11

Knock, Knock…

So, you really want go through the door? You've read it and you get the point, and, "All right already, let's get on with it. What's the catch? What does it take? How does it work? What's going to happen?" You're excited and you want to know why it took so long to get to the point!

In fact, we have been pointing to it all along, and some will have gotten it. It could have been stated in the short version in about three words. The reason for the long preamble though, is that while I am talking to you, I know that the Tags are listening too. They will think of all sorts of things to make you feel and judge what has been written in such a way that you will want to dismiss it. Some will complain that it is not scientific enough. Others – that it is not spiritual enough. Yet others, that it is too long, short, etc., etc. What about that person who's Tags were so great that he or she didn't even pick up the book for x number of Tag reasons!

You have gotten this far – congratulations. You must realize by now that there is a big difference between looking at your doors and going through them. Your Tags may let you see that there is a door, but there are many people like the client of mine who said, "I know it is what I should do, and want to do, but I'm just too afraid to try." Actually, taking the step through the door requires a special thing to happen. It requires that you invoke the most human part of you, that which separates you from your animal cousins, that which says you are human – your Will.

I have said a few times already that it is simple to go through the door, but I know it is not easy while your Tags are so compelling. The actual steps to take are not difficult, but what will go on in your mind, body and spirit, as you take your steps, well, that is when your Will needs to be strong. That is when your Tags will scream at you, make you apathetic, or your heart pound; will fill your blood full of adrenaline as if you were facing a dragon, and well, maybe you are!

"THROUGH THE DOOR!"

Your preconditioned response to change is a pattern that is so set that you automatically go there.

Whenever I hear someone say that people can't really change, I cringe. That statement is only true when people meekly follow the dictates of their Tags. When in autopilot, and that's what Tags are, you can expect to be taken where the compass has been set. But humans can always will a change of course. Are you ready to take the helm? Are you ready for the consequences, because there will be some. It will change your life. After all, that's what you wanted in the first place when you picked up this book, but are you ready to accept those changes?

Whether we are taking about letting yourself increase your productivity as a salesperson, change your career, do your job better, lose weight, get fit, say no, say yes, travel around the world, ask for a raise, get married, get divorced, leave home, go home, say you're sorry, say you're angry, or simply deciding to be happy… whatever it may be, it requires a walk through the door. It requires you to change direction in spite of everything and everyone, including your own whining inner dialogue that tells you different. But what about the Tags that say you don't deserve better, or can't do better? Are you ready to dump those in the garbage? I know you can. I know you deserve to.

When you go through the door, what will you find? You will find yourself in a corridor full of doors. These will all be doors offering you choice. Some will make a little difference in your life, some will be major, and all will be an expression of who you are. Your life can be a series of open doors. For every new adventure, every time you do something out of conscious choice, a door is opened.

Invoking Your Will

Invoking your Will is a process that happens only in the presence of a conscious mind. When you put on your shoes, something that you have done so many times in the past, most of the activity is done unconsciously. In effect, you are not present for most of the task, and it is not an act of Will but an act by rote. Invoking your Will is a declaration of intent. It is the declaration of a conscious decision. The word "decision" has at its root the connotation of cutting something off. Therefore, to decide on one thing is to cut off other options from the menu of choice.

Invoking your Will, then, is a decision that the path to take is the one and only path at that particular time and the ensuing consequences of that path are accepted even if not liked. The act of invoking your Will brings an immediate response from Tags whose mandates are the preservation of the authority invested in them to control your behaviour.

Know now that the stronger the Tag you wish to overcome, the greater it will fight back!

An example here will help us understand the process as it unfolds.

Weight is the one topic so many people are talking about, and it certainly is a highly visible Tag solution. The number of people not only overweight but also obese in North America, is staggering and the numbers are climbing. So, in this discussion, it is safe to say that we can talk to a good number of people who will be in a position to react to the statements I am going to make. The reactions are important, so I wish to target as large a group (no pun intended) as possible.

Those of you who are not overweight can easily think of someone you know who is and imagine how they would feel at these words. You may still be triggered if you have a loved one in this situation. It is very important that you pay attention to how your feelings are going to change while you read this. Don't go too fast because I want you to remain conscious of the fact that what I am about to say will seem like an attack to your Tags. It is important to remember that the Tags are not you. They are the instructions you have learned from out there, on how you should think and act, based upon on the criteria that your tribe has decided. Tags control your behaviour by evoking emotions that will effectively move you away from any action that would cause you to go directly against the Tag's view of how you should behave. You should realize that your Tags are already on red alert because of this preamble, and consequently, are ever so vigilant.

I'll tell you plainly and simply why I think, you are overweight. It's not important to discuss the mechanics of excess weight, in others words, how you got weighty. I am going to tell you simply why you got overweight. Deepak Chopra brilliantly talks succinctly about the difference between the "…mechanisms of disease vs. the origins of disease." Thus, the rational arguments of how you became that way physically merely indicate the method, not the reason. So yes, the diet of most people is atrocious, the food is all laced with everything that isn't good for us, we eat too much, too fast, etc., etc., but having said all that, understand that the culture is set up that way so that these conditions exist. In other words, the tribe has set up the system where the Tags may work for the tribe's good.

Some of you are steeling yourself for something threatening that you think is coming up. Can you sense this? If you are saying to yourself, "What's he going to say next?" what is your tone of voice in your head when this question arises? Is it defensive, angry, or even frightened? You might want to write down how your feelings are changing while reading what's coming up next. This is going to require a high level of honesty on your part, but most importantly, it will require that you observe your changes in thought, emotions and even your physical posture and comfort. Be present!

Your body has incredible resources for regeneration and capacities to maintain optimal health. Athletes break limbs and in a couple of months, they're back at their sport. Accident victims are torn up but the body mends. This wonderful stuff we are made of knows how to keep itself in great condition. If it has deviated from that course, it is then following the dictates of a senior advantage. With the absence of The Will to choose consciously something different, Tags, whose mandates are established and frozen in time, will dictate this senior advantage. Therefore, an excess weight gain is satisfying your present strongest image of yourself. In other words, you're fat because your Tags, for their own reason, want or need you to be! If your weight keeps you from being loved, then your Tags see being loved as anti whom you are, and will use the weight to try to prevent it. If the weight keeps you unhappy, then happiness is something your Tags have deemed not in your best interest. Whatever you lose by being in this condition is precisely what your Tags are working hard to keep you from having. From the viewpoint of the Tags, that which you lose is that which is "unsafe" for you to have. You are walking around with what you call "self-images" that want you to be fat to keep you from being happy, or healthy, confident, etc.

Right about now, many of you will be discounting completely what I have just said. Your Tags will have been triggered by these statements and would naturally be needful of attacking them. Making you feel superior, condescending, and especially defensive would be my guess for the most triggered feelings that are coming up in many of you now who are overweight. Most of you would argue, quite forcefully, I'm sure, that there is no way in hell that you actually want to be overweight! You might be doing all sorts of things to get the weight off and are really struggling so much that what I'm saying seems insulting or just plain cruel. The very thought of someone telling you that you are that way because a part of you wants or needs to be, is ludicrous, given all the effort some of you go into preventing it or reversing it.

Before you justify your feelings by saying that, you are simply sure that I am wrong, and it has nothing to do with Tags, think about it. There is a difference between an intellectual disagreement, and an emotional response to an idea. The defensive emotions supply you with plenty of armour, but very little in the way of solutions. That's because being over-weight is a solution. It just happens to be a problem with the battles between your inner senses of who you would like to be, which is of little consequence to the Tags. In other words, the battle is between Will and Tags. Therefore, for most of you, the weight stays on.

What has happened in the past when you have tried to lose weight? You geared yourself up for an ordeal of deprivation. You talked yourself into shame for the shape you were in and emotionally pushed yourself to get into shape. Maybe you were more positive and took a gentler approach to yourself, with pep talks and promises of rewards if you got down to a certain weight. You skipped meals, starved yourself or bought any number of products used for meal replacements. After a lot of work and time, the weight went down and you were happy.

Then what happened?

Maybe you went out with some friends to a nice restaurant where they were serving some great desserts where you thought, "What the hell? Just once," and then one thing led to another and the next thing you knew, the weight was back up there again. Something happened and happens to everyone in these situations. They say things like, "I couldn't help myself," or, "I just wasn't thinking."

Another scenario is the one where ever so slowly you ate a little bit more each time until the weight crept back up to where it was. In other words, in spite of the desire to reach a certain goal, a certain level of unconsciousness crept in and you "found yourself" in a behaviour pattern that automatically brought you back to where you were, if not even more overweight.

Many of you have tried some of the countless available diets, but have not increased the exercise necessary to get fit because it meant others seeing you in workout clothes. We certainly know that we have Tags for how we look and what is acceptable in our tribe for us to be deemed presentable.

There are several types of Tags that have the ability to cause an overweight condition. Overweight problems are the direct result of Tags. In other words, the weight problem is, in fact, a Tag's solution to what the Tag learned about you and your relation to certain other people. (Lest you feel particularly singled out, virtually all problems with the physical body are solutions the Tags have found to maintaining their existence.) The effect of the excess weight a person carries is that of literally insulating themselves from the outside world. Depending on the exact Tag, it functions to keep people away ("because people hurt me," or, "I don't deserve the love and attention that others get"). It can also keep you from certain activities ("because I might get hurt doing that").

There are a few more beliefs or Tags that could use excess weight as a means of maintaining the Tag's image of it self, but your weight is there mostly due to a Tag in your mind. In other words, a Tag believes very strongly that the excess weight is exactly what you need, and dutifully furnishes you with it. Weight, therefore, is a Tag solution that maintains the Tag image.

Here is the reason why weight was selected as an example. When I see so many people in this condition, and obviously, it is a very visible condition, it tells me that there are many people unhappy out there.

KNOCK, KNOCK...

When you listen to the infomercials of weight-loss advertisers and pay attention to the endorsements, you hear of people telling us how unhappy they were, and how ashamed they were of themselves and their weight. It is actually the other way around. They were unhappy and ashamed of themselves so they put on the weight. The individuals, finally having enough, decide to invoke their Will and do something rather than letting the Tags produce the "safe" behaviour.

The world is not an unhappy place. We have far more capacity for happiness and success than we could even imagine. Our species has been more interested in the survival of itself than the needs of the individual, and societies around the world have been built up around that evolutionary urge.

I know that many of you have read other books relating to self-awareness. If you have caught glimpses of the works of people such as Deepak Chopra, Wayne Dyer, Caroline Myss, and Gary Zukav, you already have a sense that what I'm saying has some validity. Yet, even knowing this, some of you still don't weigh what is reasonable for your body, or live the life that fulfills you.

What manner of Tag is so comfortable with its own power over you that it can stand boldly in front of you knowing that it is safe from your Will to change it? Some of the most insidious emotions that Tags can bestow on you are apathy or indifference, for they zap you quietly of your energy and Will Power to move into action. As a society/tribe, our Tags have filled us with such thoughts of impotence that we would rather accept the "hits" of sugar, sex, chocolate, sounds, and smells that society offers, than choose a different direction called upon by our own spirit!

The idea that our illnesses and problems are caused by our thinking is not earth shattering by any means. I'm neither the first, nor the last person to suggest this, either. What I am putting forth is the idea that the Tag has an evolutionary need to exist and exert its influence on your thinking any way it can. If a debilitating, physical condition will solve the "greater problem" of survival, than it is always a viable option for the Tag to implement it to solve the problem. Your desires are secondary to the Tag's need to take care of you in its own way. The Tags have, of course, given you other things to think of, or created situations whereby the relative importance of your desires is diminished. Remember that the Tags are part of a system of the brain that has kept our species alive and flourishing for a long time, so they know how to distract you from your goals. Tag goals are automatic and always active, whereby your wishes and desires are the product of conscious thoughts that are sometimes indecisive and fleeting.

It is guaranteed that invoking your Will and going against the dictates of your Tags will cause your fears, embarrassments, shame, whatever the hook is, to be amplified. Just thinking of losing weight for some people causes stress and can cause some to binge for the fear of becoming perpetually hungry. (Is there a great feeling of lack hidden there somewhere?)

What people really want is a way to get what they want without having to be so afraid to go through with it. Well, you must know by now that it doesn't work that way. The fear is there in order to stop you, not because of a real danger; rather it is a Tag's perception of its own predicament.

To experience first hand what I'm talking about, go to a karaoke bar and then, sitting there amid the crowd, start contemplating actually getting up and singing in front of all the people!

This is not an intellectual exercise; I strongly suggest that you actually do this in order to feel the Tag in the moment. Especially for those of you not affected by the weight discussion above, this exercise can be your in-your-face introduction to one of those great Tags that most people have. Reach over and grab the booklet or paper or whatever they have in the bar that lists the songs on it. Grab the pencil as if to write something. Now some of you are going to have an extremely hard time doing just this because it will mean that some people near you are going to think that you want to go up and sing, and that alone will be too much for you. Of course, those of you who do karaoke all the time won't get the same feelings, but there are enough of you out there who wouldn't be caught dead singing to a group of strangers; and you will experience what I am explaining. The rest will know someone who would.

Tags can be triggered in most of you with this one. If you're like many people, you will start to sweat at the very idea of singing on stage.

KNOCK, KNOCK...

While you are watching others going up there, you will notice that the singers are actually cheered, no matter how well or badly they sing, so there is no real danger. If anything, there is admiration and support. So why are you so afraid? Nothing is going to hurt you and if anything, you will be a hero to all the others who are too afraid to go up. No, the fear is not based on any real danger at all. You can say that you don't want to make a fool of yourself, you can't sing, and you'll look like an idiot.

Yet it is not "looking like an idiot" that is the problem.

You let your Tags stop you because of the fear of how you are going to feel while you are up there. You must understand this fundamental difference. Those feelings going on in your mind as you merely sit there and contemplate going up to the front and singing. It is these feelings you avoid at all costs.

Those shadows we've talked about in "Shadowboxing", the decoys, allow you to live in a world of imagined threat. The battle is not a battle of the interactions with your peers; it is the interaction between self and Tags. It is a battle that goes on in an interior world, but plays out on an exterior stage.

Most of the things that you have feared in your life have never happened. Of those that did, most were handled in such a way that little scars have been left behind emotionally or otherwise. Yet, the day-by-day worries for non-happening events exact a toll on your entire physical and mental well-being. Your Tags are so guarded for every potential disaster that might befall any one of them that the bulk of your energy is spent circumventing the impending feelings that any of these Tags might threaten you with.

You are not normally conscious of this because the mind ceases broadcasting to you to conscious information of continuous events. That is why ten minutes after walking into a room that smells bad you no longer smell the odour. It doesn't disappear; it just becomes a baseline that the brain doesn't bother telling you about. So too, the continuous reactions to your fears are not even noticed, even though an outsider looking at you could spot it in a second.

So let's put you back at karaoke night. It's time to go through the door! You're sitting there and embarrassed as hell at the thought of going up. Especially since some overweight old guy just got up and sang just like Elvis Presley. (Hey, could it be…Nah.) The Tag shadows you are feeling at this moment are your biggest concern.

Realize this right now, for the last time:

It is the feelings (in this case they can range from mild embarrassment to outright fear) which you want to avoid at all costs, not the actual situation. The actual situation is an internal one. The circumstances and individuals in the external scenario matter only in how they trigger the inner situation – the confrontation with the Tag. You are being threatened by these feelings and you hate them with a passion. Many things can trigger them, but right now, it's the idea of getting up in front of these people and actually singing.

You are living the Tag experience!

Do those Tags have anything to do with you? Courage, folks, say: "NO!"

Are those Tags creating artificial fears? (Is anyone being killed for singing?) Just say: "NO."

Do you owe any allegiance to these Tags? Don't forget to breathe people, and say… "NO."

Then, if you owe nothing to the Tags, you need not listen to their messengers, the shadows called Tag-feelings. They won't just go away; I'll say that repeatedly. They are doing their perceived job, but you don't have to listen to them. They are not natural warnings or intuitions or gut feelings that require your attention. They are shadows of something others tried to convince you were important – but they are not.

The door is right where you are. When you get up and sing, you will be going through it. You will actually be going against the Tag that serves up bad feelings to keep you in check. This is how you go through a door, and this is a fine example of one. Who you are is important. What you have to say is important. Your feelings, not the Tag's garbage, but your real self's feelings can be untainted by the games played to make you feel less than what you are. They are so important and not to be discouraged, ever. Find a song that expresses some of what you feel and get up there and do it!

KNOCK, KNOCK...

Of course, you are scared, sweating, dry-mouthed, and knock-kneed. So? That is what Tags do. You do it in spite of all of this. Don't fight shadows – that only makes them stronger. Go through the door and out the other side. Never let your Tags silence you again!

Just so that you are, clear on this, when you do it, and I hope that you do go through this door, it doesn't mean that the very next time you're in this situation that you won't feel the exact same way. Remember, the Tags don't just go away.

Depending on the intensity of the Tags, or rather, how strongly they were given to you, they will take a lot of convincing that you are safe in this situation before they relax their guard and stop sending in the troops to protect you.

My goal here is quite simply to get as many people as possible all over the world, (yes, I'm ambitious but determined) to get up and express themselves just like they did when in their childhood at a very early age; then there was no such thing as pain and suffering for just being you. You yelled, screamed, laughed, cried and sang at the top of your voice, just for the sheer joy of hearing yourself. You didn't feel stupid for you didn't even know what the word meant. You certainly were not ashamed of your voice – hell no! It was your first toy!

This is but one example of going "through the door". Many of you saw the film The Wizard of Oz, based on Frank L. Baum's series of books. The movie, you will remember, starts out in black and white. When the tornado sets the house down unscathed and then Dorothy opens the door to go outside, the movie changes to full colour so that the view inside the cabin is in black and white, but through the door, it is in colour.

The transition to colour, which contrasted greatly from the dreary black and white landscape of Kansas, caused Dorothy to utter that oft-quoted line: "*Toto, I've a feeling we're not in Kansas anymore.*" I never forgot this scene, maybe because it was so dramatic at the time.

When I realized the process of defying the Tags and then acting contrary to the feelings with which the Tags were clawing me, the sensation of that realization was like that moment in the movie when Dorothy went through the door. Realization does change the landscape of our lives. Sensations are amplified tenfold because the ones we are feeling are ours. They are our true feelings and not those phoney ones pretending to be our friends.

In Neale Walsch's book, Conversations with God – Book 2 (1997), we have God (who knows), telling the author,

"The soul speaks to you in feelings. Listen to your feelings. Follow your feelings. Honour your feelings."

Here "God" is giving the author the simple message of how to express oneself and find glory in the life we live, by listening to our feelings. There is no conflict with what I am saying here when I call the emotions of guilt, shame, embarrassment and unrealistic fear, Tag-feelings. Do not listen to them. These are not the same things as our feelings. Fortunately, in the same book, a few pages later, "God" says,

"Some feelings are true feelings – that is, feelings born of the soul – and some feelings are counterfeit feelings, these are constructed in your mind." (Walsch, 1997)

Be conscious of the difference! How do we know the difference? Our souls have no need to speak to us in such a way as to give us Tag-feelings. Tag-feelings are born in the mind that has been programmed to obey certain rules of the tribe or face the consequences of feeling the lash on its back. As Tag-feelings dig into our skin keeping us in check from being too much of our self, we become predictable, consistent and controllable.

We are much more than this. And in those quiet moments when the chatter of the world is stilled, we hear that faint whisper, which beckons us to follow our hearts and do that which truly makes us happy. Then the messenger is our inner self, or as some may call it, our Soul. It calls us to go through one door after another, doors of experience where we can stretch out unencumbered and express our individuality. In these moments, we will know our self and the searcher and searched become one.

So clearly going "through the door" is an act of courage. It is a heroic dragon slaying, save the damsel, free the slaves, act that breaks the chains around your ankles and lets you move forward. It ceases to be a question of "how do I get rid of the fear that stops me", and becomes a statement of, "In spite of the fear, I move forward".

12

"The Keys, Please!"

The document that establishes what happens to our property after we are dead is a Will. As in, "When I'm dead, you will get the house, the stereo, and my Beatles Album collection!" The context of the word Will, here, suggest its original meaning, to wish, to want. In this context, the word accurately expresses the intent.

A casual look in any dictionary will expose the fact that the word will has several meanings and expresses present as well as future ideas. Often in our speech, we use the word will as a means of diverting action and decision

Think of how many times someone has said to you:

"Let's get together soon.", and you reply:

"Yeah, we will, real soon..." with no intention of doing so. Imagine that you are looking at something in a store and when the clerk pushes you a little towards the sale, you tell her that you will be back later when you have more time, or when your husband is with you, knowing full well that you will never return.

You use the word Will often as a promissory statement knowing that the promise will remain unfulfilled. You do this because it somehow saves face, and keeps us you from saying what you truly mean – "I'm not coming back ever because the food was awful!" or "This is way too expensive for my budget."

We have manipulated the word will in our everyday speech such that it tends to be:

- In the future,
- Changeable,
- Holds little promise of truth or completion,
- Often related to things to which we ascribe little meaning.

Now imagine yourself putting faith in your Will Power under these circumstances!

I hope that you now realize that you have a Tag associated with the word Will. Predictably, it seems insane for me to advocate to you to invoke your Will when the word itself is stripped of all its power to invoke the idea strength and victory. You should also be getting the idea that if you want to tap into the most powerful tool in your mind, you had better have a word for it that is not confused with, imbued with, or otherwise tainted with, anything that may have a less than powerful association. The word must not only be powerful, you must sense that it is a power that you can access freely. Then and only then will it be a tool at your conscious command. It should conjure in your mind the idea of power and "now". It needs to elicit from you the unfettered ability to choose freely without compromise.

> NOTE: In the rest of this chapter, I will use "him and her" interchangeably, even in the same sentence. Some of you are men, some are women, and I want you to be able to picture an aspect of yourself as I am writing and I want to be sure that you sense the truth; that I'm talking to you personally.

I am going to suggest that you substitute the word, "Commander" for Will. A commander, by definition is the person in charge. A commander does not ask permission. A commander has resources at his command. A commander is used to getting things done, and has full expectation of the fruition of her wishes.

The word commander should elicit within you a strong image. Do not think of any commander that you may have known or read about, for there were some commanders who lost in battle, or made foolish mistakes. This is not the commander of your mind. Get the idea in your mind of an idealized commander. Picture him as strong and unflinching. She is an in command by competence rather than position, type of individual. She is not afraid of making mistakes, is not stopped by fear, nor intimidated by shame and guilt. He is steadfast and unwavering by doing what is right without compromise. Your commander is a leader, admired and respected by others. Being a real commander, he need not dominate others, show off, or seek rewards at other people's expense. Being a real leader means that her self-esteem is solid, therefore she does not need to compare herself with others to define who she is. He does not need to diminish others to seem superior. He is superior to his fears and other feelings that would hold her back, and that is power enough.

Your Commander is so strong that he does not need to waste time fighting a Tag that tries to hold him back. The Commander is aware of the Tag's presence but has no need to fight it. The Tag is not that significant to a commander because the Commander always knows she is in charge.

What I have described is, in fact, a description of your Will. This is exactly the command capacity of your Will. You may not have thought of it in these terms, and that is precisely why we must rename it so that it can only evoke an image that is positive and clearly not confused with future promises that you will not keep.

There is one more association you have to make. We have described the Commander, and you probably have a mental picture of her in your mind. If the Commander is the person in charge, and you understand the idea of invoking your Will, then what you are really doing is putting the Commander to work. Yet, wait a minute; the Commander is in charge, so how can you put him to work? Easy, you are the Commander-in-Chief! You are the Commander's Commander. You tell your Commander what to do, and then you know that it will happen, because that is the only option.

We are not creating a new thing here. The commander was always there, and you have always been the commander-in-chief. You may not have been conscious of the power of your Will, and you may not have separated your self-images among the ones that you created and the ones created outside of yourself.

I have described processes, given them names and pictures you can see. You have an idea as to how it works, and why it so often appears not to work. Essentially, we are getting the language right. Let us further clarify the essence of meaning here to paint as clear a picture as possible of what we are doing.

Right now wherever you are, please raise your arm and then put it back down.

(No, I mean it! Just raise it up and put it down.)

I'll wait…

"THROUGH THE DOOR!"

Our imprecise language says that you raised your arm, but the arm is you or a part of you. By the same process, you invoke your Will or call the Commander to act, but you are the Commander. Your arm does as commanded, and it behaves just as it should – as an arm. You cannot ask it to digest your food for you. Similarly, the Commander must act like a Commander. It cannot do otherwise.

That is what makes the Commander so powerful. If you find yourself in a situation where you want to create a life change, make your Commander do it! Being shy does not bother her. If you want to quit your job to start up your own business, but are afraid to, get your Commander to do it. He will not let fear get in the way.

Start getting the idea that your Commander is as available to you as your legs are when it is time to walk. The only difference is that you are so used to using your legs that you no longer pay attention to the command you give them to walk. They just seem to do it without being told to – but you do command them!

Next, you need to visualize your Commander. Calling your Will a Commander has significantly changed your emotional and mental view of it. The word Commander elicits a response different from the word Will. Just think of saying something to yourself as simple as:

"I will tell him exactly what I think."

Now compare that with this:

"I command myself to tell him what I think!"

Feel the difference? That's the power of the right word for the right situation.

What does your Commander look like? What do you think he or she should look like? For one thing, she should look invincible. When you see her face, it should radiate quiet confidence. The expression on your Commander's face should leave you no doubt as to her strength of purpose. This is the person whom you would have loved to come rescue you from antagonizing bullies. He would simply have to walk up behind you and the bullies would run away.

Get the picture?

Quiet strength.

"THE KEYS, PLEASE!"

What does your Commander sound like? Have you ever heard someone talk, and just the sound of his or her voice commanded attention? If you have heard such a person, you will realize that it was not because she was so loud, or in your face when he spoke; rather it was probably a voice of quiet assurance; a voice that spoke from an unwavering knowledge of purpose and intent. The body language of the person was completely congruent with the words that she spoke. The words were uttered as truths without hurry in the voice, or high-pitched tension; only the quiet power of assuredness.

That is how your Commander speaks.

You know that the difference between a Tag and a true self-image is that Tags were someone else's view of who you are, superimposed over your own view making it hard for you to see through your own image. The self-image itself is how you see yourself.

With that in mind, create your Commander.

I have given you ideas as to how he might look, and what qualities would be effective for you; but you create her to your own image! Just make your Commander a person who gets things done for you.

Take the time to create your Commander. Make him so real that you could swear that she is walking behind you all the time. (In truth, he always was; you just didn't pay attention.) Get as clear an image as you can of your Commander's looks, voice, mannerisms, and sense the power that is contained there. This self-image can eat Tags for breakfast!

You need to practice putting the Commander to work, and paying attention to the fact that it does indeed work for you. Do it enough and you will find that your whole outlook on life has changed because you are less and less hampered by the feelings or shadows of Tags. Again, realize that this does not mean that neither the Tags nor their feelings go away. It just means that you pay less and less attention to them.

We will get into the specifics of how we do this in the next chapter. The result of putting your commander to work is that you start to feel a sense of power within you. You see yourself doing more and reaping the benefits of living your life and not someone else's view of what it should be. You are now in command!

In Hindu mythology, certain gods came to earth as personalities to interact with the world. It is said that the god Vishnu came to earth as Krishna whom we read of in the Bhagavad-Gita. The term used to express the personification or incarnation of a god on earth is an Avatar.

It is fascinating to observe the context in which the idea of an avatar is playing on the internet. People are creating cyber-worlds and filling them with personifications of themselves in order to move within these fantasy worlds. People create icons called avatar so that the world at large sees an image of the internet user that is more in keeping with the ideal that the user has of him or her self. More often than not, the image of the avatar looks more like the ideal image the person has of him or herself than an actual physical likeness. The anonymity provided by the internet removes the need for factualism and allows the internet user the ability to project ideas and images of themselves that they would desire to possess.

What they have inadvertently created is a cyber-commander that can manifest the Will itself albeit in a limited fashion. It is unfortunate that most of these individuals have latched on to a great idea only to use it in its least powerful capacity. The mind makes no distinction between the imagined and the so-called real world. I want to stress here that you again for the last time that the world in your mind affects you exactly the same way as the world out there. Do whatever reading it takes to convince you of that. Read the books suggested in the bibliography and get yourself to the point were you can truly understand this mind-body connection. Your commander is an avatar; a personification of godhood if you like, that which embodies the essence of what is really you devoid of tribal influence and the means of perfect self-expression.

We are now at another door. Your "command" of what I am saying here determines whether it opens or not. This is the precise point where one or more of your Tags are going to go into red alert. You now have a key to a door and an invitation to walk through it.

If anything is to trigger a Tag to react, this is it. So pay attention to your feelings right now! If what I've just described seems stupid, crazy, or just plain foolish, you must ask yourself why. If you find some way of dismissing the Commander as being too easy, too difficult, or too silly to do, you need to ask yourself why.

Remember that feelings are the shadows cast by Tags. They make you focus on the shadow so that you do not pay attention to the Tags trying to stop you from changing. Many of you at this point will be tempted to start shadowboxing; that is, working on the feelings that building a strong image of your Commander is just a silly exercise, or some trick. You will want to dismiss this exercise as a foolish activity. For those of you who intellectualize yourself from passing through the door, I distinctly heard your Tags yell out, "Gottcha!" What do you have to lose from trying?

For those of you, who have walked through the door, welcome to the new room. Before we go on to the next chapter, spend whatever time it takes to build your image of your Commander. Don't read anymore until you can see, feel, taste, and touch your Commander. She will have work to do, and there is no room for failure. Build him and I'll wait for you in the next chapter.

13

The Walkabout

I would not expect anyone to be able to drive a car well the first time he or she got behind the wheel. There are just too many things to do and concentrate on. Similarly, I would not expect you to charge into the world with your Commander at your side, knowing exactly what to do, without a few tests first. What we will do then is show you what your Commander can do for you through a small door before you head out on the main gateway!

I am going to have to assume that you are able to visualize your Commander with ease. If you are one of the few people who are not that visual and have a hard time picturing your Commander, then your responsibility is to accept the fact that even though you can't see her, she is there, as large as life and standing right behind you. Know that everyone else can sense him and is responding to his presence. When I first created my commander, I could not come up with the image I wanted. No human face seemed to do it for me. What I saw in my mind was an aura of scintillating lights about the size of a large person. These lights didn't speak but imparted the complete sense of everything that I would call a commander. Eventually I came up with a physical persona that was acceptable to me. So if you happen to be like me, don't sweat the image. The most important thing is your trust in the capacity of your commander to command!

What you are going to do now is go on a walkabout. That is, you are going to go for a walk along Main Street, or through the local Mall, or any other place where there are many people about. You will walk along the street or Mall and this time, you are going to start paying for your new associate, the Commander.

You will pay attention to the fact that she is right there with you. You will pay attention to fact that everyone around you is aware that the Commander is right with you. You will pay attention to the difference this makes to how you walk and talk to the people around you. Feel what it is like going into a café and ordering a cup of coffee or a cold drink and knowing that the Commander is causing others to see you in a completely different light. It is as if you are walking around with a king or queen of a great nation and everyone is aware that royalty is your friend.

As you do this, notice how your body language is different. See how you walk a little taller? Your shoulders are rotated more towards the back, giving you a wider stance. Look people in the eye as you walk past them. Let them know you are there. Give a small smile or a hint of a nod at passers-by. They are not just looking at you; rather, they are looking at you and your Commander as a formidable team. What respect that engenders! You two appear as if you could do anything. That is no threat to anyone, because others can plainly see that your strength comes without threat to anyone. You simply are a powerful, self-actualized person.

Make sure that when you open a door to let yourself into or out of a store that you allow others behind you to pass by first. Give them that knowing nod, as you let them go by, that you have all the time in the world, because the "meeting" will not start without you anyway; therefore, you can't be late. It is not arrogance that gives you a sure-footed gait; it is just that the world, being such a wonderful place, accommodates you.

Walk around with that expression on your face that simply says, "Stick with me, 'cause I'm going places!"

Pay attention to how you feel, how you walk, how others pay attention to you, how great the day really is. What's the difference?

You have not created an illusion; you have simply focused on what was always there. The skills that allowed you to drive a car with ease were always there, even when you clumsily took the wheel for the first time. You merely needed to develop the awareness of these skills and practice using them. It is the same for your awareness of the Commander. He was always there to back you up in any situation, you just never turned around to look and see if he was there. In addition, because you are the Commander-in-Chief, the Commander will not act until given a direct command from you. Once given, you need do nothing else. The Commander will take full charge.

Do your Walkabout as often as needed for you to know that you are, in fact, the Commander-in-Chief. When you can command that feeling at will, you will be able to go on to the next step – sending your Commander on an assignment.

Those of you who wonder whether everything in this chapter sounds just too crazy for words, then I suggest you go back and reread Chapter 9. You must get it into your belief systems that what your mind conceives is just as real as what it sees in the outside world.

Why in the world do you get scared watching a horror movie? It is just lights hitting on a white wall, and sound coming out of speakers. You know that, and yet you still get some strong emotional response from watching the movie. In spite of what you know to be true, your mind and body responds to the reality of the fiction.

Your mind's ability to make movies real is why you go to them; or else the idea of sitting there and responding strongly to lights on a wall would be too ridiculous to comprehend.

Don't make the mistake of thinking of this as role-playing. It isn't. You are merely activating what you already have. You've done it before; you just didn't have a name for it, nor were you conscious of it. Now it has a name and that name is the Commander. You are indeed the Commander-in-Chief.

14

The Assignment

I know you have completed the Walkabout because you certainly don't want your Tags taking over at this point after all the time you've spent reading this. If you were settled down to read and you came to this chapter and thought that you'll just read on and see what it says – STOP! Don't do it. You must do your Walkabout before you read on. Make the decision not to stand on the sidelines and watch others do while you just stand there. This is not theoretical. Anything else is Tag behaviour. Invoke your Will, take your Commander out for a stroll, and then come back here. We will all wait for you.

As I was saying before, now you have taken the Commander out for a walk, introduced him to the world and it felt great.

You now know that you have a resource that you can tap into that will give you strength that everyone can feel. You have felt the way it makes you walk taller, and with more confidence.

Now it is time to send the Commander on a small errand. The task is up to you, but here is a possible list from where you may select the errand:

- There is someone you want to say something to, but are too shy, nervous, timid, etc.
- There is a small task you need to do, but you have put it off because it made you feel intimidated. (These things would include asking someone to pay back money they owe you, apologizing to someone for something you said/did, or asking for an apology from someone.
- There is an item of clothing you wanted to wear, but didn't have the nerve to put it on.
- You have wanted to cut your hair, change you hairstyle or colour dramatically, but were too intimidated to do it before.

"THROUGH THE DOOR!"

Something along those lines is waiting for you. I don't know what it is, but we all have some things that we have put off because it was "easier" to put off than to think about. Pick one!

Get something in your mind that needs or wants saying or doing. The truth is, you know it has not been done because some sort of Tag feeling was keeping you from doing it. It may have been guilt, shame, embarrassment, shyness, or anything else along these lines. You get the idea.

It is important now that you get one of these tasks firmly in your mind. What is it you need to say or do? Now you simply tell your Commander what it is you want done. Do it clearly. For example:

"Jim borrowed some money from me 6 weeks ago. He said that he would pay me back 'next week'. He hasn't said anything to me one way or the other and that just isn't right."

"Commander, you take charge. I want you to call him and tell him that I'm really disappointed that he not only hasn't paid me back , but didn't even have the courtesy to tell me what was going on. Find out what is going on, and what he intends to do about it."

With the task clearly in mind, and your Commander briefed on exactly what she is supposed to do, let her make the call for you. It isn't relevant that you are doing the dialling and it is your voice Jim is going to hear; your Commander will do the talking. It is perfectly okay that Jim thinks that it is you talking. That is exactly what you want him to think. You have been too shy, embarrassed, or intimidated to do it, and you know that you were just shadowboxing.

You are doing what you must do, and your Commander is helping you. Get ready. Get your task clear in your mind; explain it clearly to the Commander.

Just one more thing – and please understand this!

The shadows cast by your Tags do not affect the Commander. Those feelings that make you cringe and cower do not affect the Commander. Shadows will continue to bother you for a while. Even though this assignment is nothing for your Commander to accomplish, it may generate in you the feelings that stopped you from doing what you wanted to do in the first place. The feelings do not go away just because the Commander is now in charge. The Tags will certainly

108

attempt to stop you from sending your Commander out to work because they know that guilt, shyness, or any other shadows thrown at you by the Tags, do not affect the Commander. You are the target of the shadows, not the Commander. That is why these feelings are directed at you.

You may already be feeling apprehensive at the thought of carrying out this task. How do you feel now? Are you nervous or afraid? Is the thought of you picking up the phone, (even though it is the Commander doing the calling) frightening to you?

That is just the way it works. The Tags are supposed to make you feel that way. That is their job. You can and should expect it to come at you with all it has. The Tags see you as having a way out and that is threatening to the way Tag's function. Your job is to decide that what you want is worth more than how the Tags are going to make you feel. Your job is to acknowledge to yourself that, in spite of how you may feel, those feelings have nothing to do with who you are and what you want.

You have your assignment. Go accomplish it now and come back here when you are done.

15

What a Day for a Daydream

Question: How do you eat an Elephant?
Answer: One bite at a time!

The first time that I consciously took my Commander out with me, I felt like a complete wimp! I could hear my Tags nagging at me and giving me all they had. I tried to rationalize how I was feeling. I felt stupid, incompetent, cowardly and just plain silly. I was the one who had labelled these feelings as Tags, I knew what was going on, and I knew what I had to do. And yet...

If your first foray into the great outdoors with your new Commander at your side was not the stellar event you hoped it would be – relax. I expected this would occur for some and it is natural if it did. Let's take the time here to look at what happened and why.

Before I go any further, those of you who had great experiences with your assignment, congratulations! Your Tags hate you already! Just kidding. Actually, it's not about our Tags hating you; I'm sure many people have Tags that get jealous at other people's good fortune. It isn't relevant because we are proud of you for getting off to a great start; now for the rest of us.

Your Tags have manipulated you all your life. They have evolved from a system that is thousands of years old and they know what they are doing. Your Will is a relatively new person on the block and has a bit of a lazy demeanour. Over the course of your life, you have not had to practice much self-awareness. There are so many opportunities to repeat the same behaviours every day that it is easy to forget that you actually have a choice! The way you eat, the way you dress, the drive to work or school; this has become routine, and routine replaces thinking.

Also, realize that everyday literally thousands of messages from the tribe bombard you as to how you should behave, what you should buy, what you should say, etc. Now you want to simply ignore all of that and live your life the way you want to. Do you think that is realistic?

I hope you answered yes.

"THROUGH THE DOOR!"

There is nothing more powerful on this earth than your Will. It does not matter how many thousands of years that Tags have been around, trying to run the show, The Will can at any time be in charge. Dressed up as the Commander, your Will is invincible.

So why did things not go as well as expected?

Because you really, really, really do not like those Tag-feelings!

You hate feeling shy, stupid, incompetent, frightened, unworthy, weak, and all those feelings that the Tags throw at you! You were just blatantly asked to go out there and do something that your Tags specifically stop you from doing, and they were not about to let you do that without a challenge. Therefore, they gave you an extra dose of feelings to try to stop this and any further action that might compromise their authority. Your Commander was waiting for you to give the word. If you think about it and are honest, you will admit that, rather than letting yourself be zapped with those feelings, you held back from actually letting the Commander get out there and do the job.

Don't worry about it; this is what you need to do. Try again. Find some smaller task if you have to, one that will not threaten the Tags too much and cause such a strong reaction. Decide now that you are going to do what you need to do, and know that the feelings will come in spite of everything. Your job is not to wait until the feelings are gone; your job is not to mind that they are there!

If you have ever sprained an ankle or had sore muscles that needed to be iced, than you know how uncomfortable ice directly on the skin can be. It is torturous in the beginning and there is nothing you would rather do than remove the ice from your skin. But — if you leave it there for at least five minutes, than you cease to feel it at all and you have no problems leaving it on for the full twenty minutes. You have, to use our symbol, gone Through the Door with the ice pack and are on the other side where the benefits are.

Therefore, you are going to have to get used to a little embarrassment, or shyness, or whatever emotion you run away from, for just a little while longer. You need to say to yourself that you are not your self-images, and those Tags have nothing to do with you. Those feelings, consequently, also have nothing to do with who you are, and although you may be feeling them, they are not telling the truth about you whatsoever.

There is a knock on your door. Someone is asking you to go out and play. What are you going to do? Do you remember those great ideas you had about something you would love to do, make, or see? Do you remember the swell of excitement that stirred within you concerning a dream you had? All of those goals, wishes, and desires; where did they come from? If they were not within your capacity to achieve, they would never have entered your mind. What stops you? Illusion. Illusion masked behind feelings controlled by that devilish puppet master, Tags.

It is a beautiful day. No matter what the weather, get your Commander out there and show the world the real you. This little book on Tags is by default a declaration of war on unconscious obedience to Tags and feelings that would seek to diminish and control you. It can change your world. You can be happier just being who you are. You can be kinder to people because the threat that Tags see around every corner won't evoke fear in you. You will be much more creative because the idea of "can't" won't come crashing down on your enthusiasm at every moment. You will find yourself being a better person, not because you fear the wrath of God and the flame of eternal damnation, but because you already are a better person than what you think you are. Without the Tags to tell you otherwise, you can just be you.

Remember that 95% of whom and what you think you are is not you, only Tags. That gives you many wonderful things to discover about yourself. What are your wishes, your longings, and your desires? Are they really that far away from possibility? Who says so? Is there any other way to get there, be there, and experience there? The world has invested much in having you behave like everyone else, but you are not everyone else – you are you. That which you have cut off to fit in with the tribe are the very limbs that would carry you to places you could hardly imagine exist.

Someone recently asked me if I believe in angels. I told him that without a shadow of doubt, I do. I see them everywhere I go and in every face that I see. Each one of you has been an angel to someone, sometime in your life. Whether it was opening a door for someone, saying a kind word at the precise moment it was needed, or lending a helping hand to someone in need. The cost of being a tribe member first and an individual second has grown over our human existence to the point where we live our lives in deficit. By invoking our Will, we lay claim to that most precious part of who we are. If avatars were the personification of the gods here on earth, than so too our true sense of self can represent the best of human nature unfettered by fears and tags born of a time when our best chance at survival was to limit ourselves to the structured demands that made a tribe work.

We are each other's guardians and the paradox is that the more you allow your true nature to shine, and the more doors you walk through, the more willingness you have to be a friend to others. Your fears cease being in charge and the power of creation, your ability to let your dreams and aspirations manifest themselves in your life becomes the most natural act of your life.

You have struggled with a weight on your shoulders. You have felt laden with guilt and fear and imagined it pressing down on you. In fact, your tag-feelings coil around your legs as they rise in devilish determination from below attempting to convince you that your dreams and aspirations are forbidden fruit. No, the weight that you carry on your shoulders is, in fact, your wings, aching to stretch and deliver you to your destiny. There is a world waiting for you to soar. All it takes is for you to go through the door.

It is time now.

Fly!

Additional Resources

Web resources:

www.Methotology.com/Through the door/html

www. Methotology.com invites you to our Forums, blogs, online discussions, and more journeys to the self. Share your "Through the Door!" stories and experiences with other, as they too journey to the self...

Send us your "Through the Door!" stories.

Going through the door will create new and wonderful journeys for you. We want to hear about your journey. In an up and coming book, we will be publishing a collection of "Through the Door!" stories as sent in by our readers. This is your opportunity to be an inspiration to others. Send your stories to:

my-journey-through-the-door@methotology.com

Bibliography

Bucke, Richard Maurice M.D. "Cosmic Consciousness" Innes and Sons (1901)

Chopra, Deepak "Quantum Healing: exploring the frontiers of mind/body medicine" New York: Bantam Books (1989)

Capra, Fritjof "The Tao of Physics: an exploration of the parallels between modern physics and Eastern mysticism" 4th ed. Boston: Shambhala Publications, Inc. (1999)

Leakey, Richard E, and Lewin, Roger "Origins: what new discoveries reveal about the emergence of our species and its possible future" New York: E P Dutton (1977)

Ornstein, Robert "The Evolution of Consciousness: the origins of the way we think" New York: Touchstone (1992)

Zukav, Gary "The Dancing Wu Li Masters" New York: William Morrow (1979)

About the Author

Phil L. Méthot is a President's Club Motivational Management consultant, lecturer, and personal development counsellor. He has worked with companies such as Air Canada, Air Transat, The Ritz Carlton Hotel, Montreal, and travelled abroad as a lecturer on Cruise Ships. He has appeared often on Radio as a guest host, and he was a leader in Eastern Canada in motivational management training. He is currently preparing a lecture tour to promote "Through the Door!" Mr. Méthot lives with his wife, Linda, in Laval, Quebec, and in their home in the Laurntians.